Rough Strength Files

ALEX ZINCHENKO

Copyright © 2014 Alex Zinchenko

All rights reserved.

ISBN: 1494750821
ISBN-13: 978-1494750824

DISCLAIMER

The exercises and advice contained within this book may be too difficult or dangerous for some people, and the reader(s) should consult a physician before engaging in them.
The author and publisher of this book are not responsible in any manner whatsoever for any injury which may occur through reading and following the instructions herein.

CONTENTS

FOREWORD	1
PREFACE	3
BASICS & METHODOLOGY	5
Why Train Rough Strength Style?	7
Progressive Resistance. Protein. Patience	12
Rough Strength Basics: How to Gain Strength?	15
Rough Strength Basics: How to Build Muscle?	19
Volume/Intensity/Frequency Relationship in Strength Training	24
Training Plan Vs Instincts	27
Full-Body Routine or Split: So What's Better?	29
Increase Your Strength with Double Progression	32
The Most Flexible Set/Repetition Scheme Ever	34
TOOLS	39
CALISTHENICS	39
Calisthenics or Weight Training – Which One Is Better?	41
Are Calisthenics Optimal for Building Muscle?	43
How to Progress Effectively in Bodyweight Exercises	46
Weighted Calisthenics: the Best of Both Worlds	53
How to Achieve the One-Arm Handstand Push-Up	56
10 Tips for Mastering the Perfect One-Arm Push-Up	67
Practical Tips to Improve Your Pull-Up Performance	75

10 Tips for Learning the Handstand	78
One-Arm Chin-Up Tips	83
Claw Fingertip Push-Ups	86
SANDBAGS	91
How to Make a Sandbag	93
5 Sandbag Strength Training Benefits	96
Sandbag Shouldering	98
How to Dominate the Sandbag Zercher Squat	103
KETTLEBELLS	111
The 5 Keys to Double Kettlebell Training	113
How to Make Your Kettlebells Heavier	115
ROUTINES	119
Mixing Training Implements for Ultimate Results	121
Top 3 Strength Routines for Beginners	127
5 x 5 Strength Training Template: How to Do It Right	132
"One Skill a Day" Training Program	138
NUTRITION	145
High-Protein Diet on a Budget	147
6 Biggest Diet Flaws	151
Supplements. Do You Really Need Them?	154
MENTAL ASPECTS	159
Your Worst Enemy	161
Why Do People Fail to Get Results?	163

Warrior Attitude to Training and Nutrition	165
Strength Training in Real Life Circumstances	168
The Main Benefit of Strength Training	173
RANDOM THOUGHTS	175
13 Random Tips on Rough Strength Training	177
The Top 5 Exercises for Awesome Shoulder Development	187
INTERVIEWS	195
Power Bar Talk with Edward of Barstarzz	197
Interview with TheSupersaiyan	202
Master Kettlebells and Dumbbells – Interview with Yahont	206
BONUS	213
The Sandbag Swing	215
3 Awesome Low-Tech Grip Exercises	218
Some Thoughts on Explosiveness	220
Which Loaded Carries to Add to Your Routine?	223
How to Avoid Wasting Time?	226
How to Make Smarter Food Choices?	228
CLOSING THOUGHTS	231
Acknowledgements	i
Recommended Reading	ii
About the Author	v
References	vi

ALEX ZINCHENKO

FOREWORD

Two athletes go through their daily training sessions.

The first one is dressed in a fluorescent vest and spandex shorts. He looks like a peacock that is trying too hard. He trains in a warm, centrally-heated gym full of padded, expensive machines. His "workouts" are built around cosmetic arm and chest exercises on those comfortable, expensive machines. In between sets, he wanders around the gym, drinks a protein shake, and generally chats and goofs around.

The workout is over when he feels "the pump".

The second wears jeans, sneakers and a black hoodie pulled over his head. He looks like some kind of dark monk. An iron monk. He does not train in a gym if he can help it. He works out in the urban environment, on the freezing, dirty concrete. He works out in silent, dusty, abandoned garages. He works out deep in the woods. His workouts are built exclusively around the most primitive, brutal methods known to our species. He hoists bone-crushing, rusted kettlebells. He manhandles unwieldy sandbags until his clothes are drenched with sweat. He performs endless pull-ups, levers and daunting gymnastics movements from makeshift horizontal bars, or from the gnarled limbs of the unforgiving trees.

The workout is over when he is a *better man* than he was before.

Let me ask you a question: which one of these two men is the *toughest*? If you yearned to quickly become stronger, leaner, more formidable and more *mentally powerful*, which one of these men would you seek guidance from?

If you said "the first guy", stop reading right now. This book is not for you.

If you said "the second guy", you are in luck. That second man is not a figure from a movie or a comic book. He is a real-life strength and conditioning coach who is causing a stir out in the Ukraine. That man is my friend, Alex Zinchenko. This is his book, his bible of strength.

Why do you need this book?

If you are sick and tired of forums overflowing with discussions of "supps, bro", "sick abz n gunz", you need this book.

If you are weary of the magazines crammed with glossy shots of physically ill, vomit-worthy steroid users, but little in the way of training science, then you need this book.

If you really ache for a deep well of useful, productive, time-tested hardcore training information, then you need this book.

If you are exhausted with the modern fake tan, chemically enhanced, lazy, pussified joke that is presented by the industry as "fitness", and you crave some real strength—*rough strength*—then congratulations, kid.

You just hit paydirt.

Paul Wade (author of "Convict Conditioning"), 2013

PREFACE

Finally, this book is ready. It was a long journey, and I am really excited to release it. There was a huge amount of work done and I seem to be finally happy with the result (if that is possible for a perfectionist).

What is the "Rough Strength Files"? Basically, it is a compilation of the 42 best articles that were written by me during the period of 2011-2013. Of course, the judge and the jury regarding "the best" status is yours truly. "2011 was long ago; didn't your views change?" – you may ask. Firstly, some things remain the same forever. Just read some classic books that were released in 18th-19th century. Many things there are still applicable to our modern high-tech life. Secondly, I rewrote many parts to make this compilation smoother and more readable.

What is the reason for this book to be published? I know that a lot of the information here is available online for free on the Rough Strength blog [1]. However, you do not always have access to the internet. This book allows you to enjoy the best articles any time you want. You can put it in your pocket, and bring it anywhere you go. In addition, you know the typical story with the blogs. You find a good blog, read a couple of articles, subscribe, and rarely come back to check out the older stuff due to lack of time or other lame reason. This book gives you the unique opportunity to have everything. Besides, it has lots of new material too.

Who is this book for? It is for all people that:
- Are sick and tired of modern fitness culture;
- Want to learn proven, real-world strength training methods that deliver results;
- Can't afford gym memberships, but have the burning desire to change;
- Are tired of all the fitness marketers out there;
- Are fond of old school physical culture;

- Want to learn how to get strong, muscular, and lean with anything you have at hand;

- Are willing to educate themselves to get better and are open to try something new.

If you are one of them, then today is your lucky day. You may have found what you were looking for.

Furthermore, **I should warn you that this is not a scientific book** (unless we are talking about bro science). So if you expect to see here research reviews, lots of heavy terminology, references to studies or other similar stuff, then you should not read it. In addition, I am not a gymnast, and not a doctor, and definitely not some kind of guru. I am just an ordinary guy who shares his experience (as well as the experiences of people who were brave enough to hire him as their coach) in strength training, nutrition, and developing mental toughness. I did my best to make all the information maximally easy for you to absorb.

Finally, most of the articles require basic knowledge of strength training terminology, so if you are a complete beginner, you may find some pieces too hard. Do not worry. Check out the "Recommended Reading" section. There will be lots of books that will help you with fundamental stuff.

That's it! Fuck long intros. Start your Rough Strength journey and enjoy the book.

Play rough!

Alex

P.S. Why exactly 42?

P.P.S. You cannot click the hyperlinks in a printed book (yep, do not even try it), that is why all of them are placed in chronological order in the "References" section in the end. You will see the actual references in the text in such style - "[1]" (no quotation marks).

BASICS & METHODOLOGY

ALEX ZINCHENKO

WHY TRAIN ROUGH STRENGTH STYLE?

There is the illimitable ocean of different training approaches out there. Why should you choose exactly the Rough Strength Method? Let us see.

What Is Rough Strength?

I want people to have clear understanding of what Rough Strength is. The word 'rough' is used here meaning not only 'hardcore', but first and foremost 'acquired without any luxuries', 'with minimum equipment'. It is a type of strength training you can perform at home with anything you have at hand.

"Hey, but isn't it the same as street workout movement or crossfit, or gymnastics, or powerlifting etc.?" Nope, it is not. You will understand that it is quite different as we dig deeper into the book.

Rough Strength is obviously not a sport (at least not at the moment of this book's release). It has a competitive edge, but that is not the main point. Why? Because it has no rules except for training for strength, progressive resistance, and minimal effective equipment. You can use any implement you have access to. Do you have nothing? Well, then there are calisthenics and gymnastic skills that will build strength just with your bodyweight. Want to add difficulty and challenge? No big deal, get a pair of rings. Want some variety but don't want to spend money on equipment? Make a sandbag. Want a versatile, interesting, and fun strength training implement? Get a kettlebell. Or better yet, pair of them. Do you have access to a barbell, dumbbells, tire, sledgehammer, gripper etc.? Awesome. Use them if you want. The rules are the same. But in the end you don't need any fancy equipment to get results. And aren't results all that matter? You can get super strong with as little equipment as bodyweight and a sandbag. So what is your excuse?

In addition, Rough Strength is more of a personal struggle to get stronger, leaner, better. It is about getting in tune with your own body. It cultivates the right attitude and discipline. It improves you as a human and a person. It is all about self-development. You and only you are the main piece of puzzle, not some unimportant things.

I will use term 'Rough Strength Method' later in this article. While there are no hard boundaries on what equipment to use, Rough Strength Method here means using calisthenics, kettlebells and sandbags separately or together as complete strength training system. These are the tools that I found the most versatile and inexpensive. Anybody can have a fully equipped home gym just with these three tools.

10 Reasons Why You Should Be Using the Rough Strength Method

1. It's almost free. I train now exclusively with three implements: rings, kettlebells and a sandbag. Although kettlebells can be pricy, I got my recent sandbag for under $5. If that is expensive for you, then training is not your thing. Go cry in pillow. Besides, calisthenics are free.

2. It's sustainable. When you have the education, you can sustain your training (and nutrition) for a lifetime. Who cares whether there is a crisis, or all gyms are closed? Or you are on an uninhabited island? Knowledge gives you freedom and sustainability. No matter what, you will always find how to train and progress further in your quest for strength.

3. It's based on facts and reasonable progressions. All of the information in this book was tested by me and my clients. I filtered useless crap, and put here only what works. In addition, I do not like just-do-it approach (used, for example, in street workout movement). If you do something, you do it on purpose. Proper programming is one of the most underrated things by regular gym rats. That is why they are so weak and girly. And that's why we are strong.

4. It builds real-world strength. Machines and bosu ball will not give you these awesome results. Strength developed with the Rough Strength method can be used anywhere: from helping your friend moving furniture to a bar fight.

5. It builds mental toughness. This is one of the most important aspects of strength training. The Rough Strength Method takes it to a whole new level. You will find out that coping with stress will be much easier. Work, family etc. If I were not training, I would have jumped off a cliff already.

6. It teaches you how to achieve "impossible" things. Progressive resistance and practice are the keys to achieving any goal or skill. Handstand, Planche, the One-Arm Chin-Up, big Bench Press, huge Squat, playing guitar, riding a bike, being a good entrepreneur etc. Make one step at a time and practice more.

7. It will help you with aesthetic goals. Who said that only barbells and dumbbells are good for getting ripped and muscular? It is all possible to achieve with calisthenics, sandbags and kettlebells, but it will take longer. Who cares in the end?

8. It can be used to supplement any sport-specific training. If you are participating in some sort of sport, then you will definitely benefit from this method. Read the reasons above. You will be stronger, leaner, more muscular, faster, more agile etc. Isn't sport about being all that and playing sport?

9. It's simple. But not easy. You concentrate only on important things and work hard to achieve them. That is how you will not waste your time. Train hard, eat right, rest, repeat. How it can be any simpler?

10. It's just awesome. Nothing to explain.

How to Use the Rough Strength Method?

First of all, who is the RS method for? It is for serious and dedicated trainees only. Regular estrogen men and gym chicks will probably find it too difficult and demanding. If you are one of the latter, stop reading right now. You will not get all the sophistication of the method, anyway. For all the others (I mean, hardcore dudes and dudettes) - read on.

To implement the Rough Strength Method, there is one important principle you need to understand: *any exercise you perform in a commercial gym can be done at home with bodyweight, sandbags, or kettlebells, you just need to find a proper substitution.* The Bench Press can be replaced with the Planche Push-Up or One-Arm Push-Up; Barbell Rows can be replaced with Front Lever Rows; Barbell Squats with Pistols or Sandbag Squats, etc. Of course, these exercises will feel different, but who cares. Again, only results matter.

To understand this more deeply, let us break down the basic categories of compound exercises:

- *Upper Body Horizontal Push* – any multi-joint exercise where your body is parallel to the ground and you are pushing the resistance away from yourself with arms. Examples: Bench Press, Push-Up, Kettlebell Floor Press etc.

- *Upper Body Vertical Push* – any multi-joint exercise where your body is perpendicular to the ground and you are pushing the resistance away from yourself with arms. Examples: Military Press, Handstand Push-Up; Dips etc.

- *Upper Body Horizontal Row* - any multi-joint exercise where your body is parallel to the ground and you are pulling the resistance to yourself with arms. Examples: Bent-Over Row, Front Lever Pull-Ups etc.

- *Upper Body Vertical Row* - any multi-joint exercise where your body is perpendicular to the ground and you are pulling the resistance to yourself with arms. Examples: Pull-Ups, Inverted Pull-Ups etc.

[With lower body everything is a bit trickier. Powerlifting-Style Squat is close to deadlifting and Sumo Stance Deadlift is close to squatting. The edge may be blurred. However, let's try to differentiate them somehow]

- *Lower Body Push (Squatting)* – any lower body multi-joint exercise where legs perform most of the work. Examples: Squats, Pistols etc.

- *Lower Body Pull (Deadlifing)* - any lower body multi-joint exercise where lower back performs most of the work. Examples: Deadlift, Good Morning, Swing.

It may be simplistic, but it works. The Bench Press, for example, is an Upper Body Horizontal Push. Now when you understand what type of movement the Bench Press is you can find a substitute for it. It can be Planche Push-Ups, One-Arm Push-Ups, Weighted Push-Ups, Kettlebell Floor Presses, Sandbag Floor Presses, etc. – the exercises from the same category.

So how to use the Rough Strength Method? Well, it all depends on your level of dedication to it. Basically, there are 3 ways:

- Incorporate exercises you like into your current routine;
- Incorporate unconventional (or home) training days;
- Use the Rough Strength Method solely.

In the first case, you will need to determine the exercise category just as we did in the Bench Press example above. After that, conventional exercise should be substituted for the one you desire.

In the second case, you can substitute the whole day of your current training program. Let us assume that the day you want to change looks like this:

A) Barbell Military Press 3 x 5
B) Barbell Bent-Over Row 3 x 6
C) Barbell Squat 3 x 8

Your Rough Strength version can look like this:

A) Sandbag Military Press 3 x 5
B) Double Kettlebell Bent-Over Row 3 x 6
C) Single-Leg Squat 3 x 8

The tricky part will be to preserve the training intensity. If you used 7-repetition maximum for Barbell Military Presses, then Sandbag Military Presses should also be performed with such intensity. You get the idea.

In the third case, you should do the same as with the second but for the whole program. When you get used to Rough Strength exercises, you will be able to create your own routines.

So which of these three ways is the best? There is no best one. All of them are viable, and everybody will find different use for the method. In the end, it all depends on individual.

Important Vs. Unimportant

Another skill you need to develop is separating the important from the unimportant. Not to bore you completely, here are two random lists.

Important:
- Progressive resistance;
- Protein;
- Discipline;
- Dedication;
- Patience;
- Consistency;
- Basic Exercises;
- Calories and Macros;
- Education etc.

Unimportant:
- Supplements;
- Equipment;
- Pump;
- Programs of Champions;
- What exercises I (or any other guy except you) use;
- Fancy gym clothes;
- Socialization;
- Ab and biceps training etc.

Closing Thoughts

That is it. Is the Rough Strength Method the only right thing to do? No. If you are doing something and it works for you, then continue doing it by all means. However, if what you are doing now does not work, you can use Rough Strength for help. If you are open-minded and ready to challenge yourself with something new, then you are welcome. Use the Rough Strength Method and get results.

PROGRESSIVE RESISTANCE. PROTEIN. PATIENCE

Are you tired of not getting results? If yes, then you are probably screwing up in one of these three fundamental principles.

Progressive Resistance

Firstly, even the most retarded gym rat should understand this. *If you are not using more weight/doing more reps/using harder exercises/doing less rest between sets/doing more sets, then you will not see any difference in your strength and the way you look.* Tattoo these words on your forehead to remind yourself of this anytime you want to change something and get weaker instead of gaining strength. Fuck, you can only do 2-3 exercises all your life and keep getting stronger in them, and you will be a powerhouse in 5-10 years. Keep getting progressively stronger in your training and you will be on the right track. Rethink your training today, make progressiveness your number one priority (not some stupid, brand new gadget or fancy exercise), and you will finally get results.

Secondly, through experience I concluded that *resistance is resistance*. Barbells, dumbbells, kettlebells, bodyweight, sandbags – they are all the same. Yes, each of them has its own pluses and minuses. But do you really think that what you are using in your training matters to your body? The right answer is no, it does not matter. Do you think that there is no way to gain muscle mass with bodyweight training? Make it progressive and work up to the hardest exercises FOR REPS (of course, you need to get your diet and rest right, which I will discuss later), and then tell me how you look. You will look big, athletic, and awesome (with a bonus of being able to control your body). The same is true for kettlebell or sandbag training enthusiast. Pick up the resistance you like, make it progressive, work up to the heaviest exercises/weights and you will be amazed with results.

Do you know why barbells are considered the king in gaining strength and size? Because it is extremely easy to make their resistance progressive with all those plates in the widest weight range possible. If it becomes easy to press a given weight, just add a couple of kilograms (or just one, or a half) and be happy. There is no need to overthink it. With bodyweight strength training, everything is WAY more complicated. Every time you move to a harder exercise, it could be a HUGE jump in resistance. For example, Handstand Push-Ups became easy and you decide to move to Diamond Handstand Push-Ups. Well, to your big surprise you are not be able to do even a single. In this case, you should try 1/2 Diamond Handstand Push-Up (or even 1/4) to make it possible. The same is true for kettlebells. You start with 16 kg, and then move up to 24 kg. Wow, it is fucking 8 kg! That is exactly why so many people fail to get results with unconventional strength training tools.

Take-home point: pick the type of resistance that you like, make it progressive, and train to success.

Protein

Protein is crucial for building muscle. Any average gym rat should know that. However, I rarely find people who want to build muscle consuming adequate amounts of protein daily. 1 g per 1 lb of bodyweight? 2 g per 1 kg? Well, this will work for *some* people, and it will be enough for people who just started training and genetically gifted population. However, for the majority it is really low number. If your training is ok (it means that you are getting stronger on a regular basis) and you consume enough calories (it means more than you burn throughout the day), but your muscles still do not grow, then you might be getting not enough protein.

What is enough? 1.5 g per 1 lb of bodyweight (3.5 g per 1 kilogram) is a good starting point. Some people will need more than that. For example, 2 g per 1 lb of bodyweight (4.5 g per 1 kilogram). These are big numbers. Still, it might be the most important diet change for you to start growing. Anyway, what will you lose if you try?

Some people can argue that you do not need so much protein, but it is highly likely that they have good genetics, or are fat bastards that think that they're muscular. These numbers are not made up from thin air. This is what works for the majority of trainees. I learned these requirements from Wesley Silveira a.k.a. Iron Addict and Charles Poliquin, as well as from some other authors who I trust. Then I checked them and was amazed with results. Do not be fooled. *You need ultra-high protein doses to grow.* Period. In addition, muscle growth is not the only positive effect of high-protein consumption. Improved fat loss is what I have noticed while experimenting. It is really insane. Increase protein intake and see for yourself.

I **do not** *recommend high-protein diet if you have kidney disease. Consult your* *doctor on this topic first.*

Side note: there are some cases when you can get away with less protein. I mean intermittent fasting and Warrior Diet. However, if you follow basic eat-whole-day approach then the numbers are accurate.

Patience

A journey of a thousand miles begins with a single step
— attributed to Lao Tzu

Patience is the third crucial factor of training (as well as any) success. What a pity that nowadays less and less people understand its importance. To achieve something valuable, you need time. I mean TIME. And lots of it. *Nobody has built great strength and physique in 4 weeks.* So why do you think that you can fully transform yours in that timeframe? There are tons of hype out there. You need to separate truth from myth. Yes, you can gain a decent amount of muscle in a short period. I've seen it, I've done it. But it is possible only in two situations:

1. You just started training and eating right.
2. You were not training and eating properly for a while and regained what you previously had due to muscle memory.

Do not search quick fixes. They will not last long. Make training, eating, and rest your new lifestyle. Only then will you be able to get the results you want. Give your goals time. *Muscle gain of 10 lb per year with consistent training is a good, solid result for an average natural trainee.* Some will be able to gain more (especially in the first year); some will gain less due to crappy genetics. Anyway, at such a pace, you will end up 30 lb (~15 kg) bigger in 3 years (this is a VERY good result; maybe for people struggling to gain muscle this number will be 20 lb (~10 kg)) An 80 kg trainee will be 95 kg and will look TOTALLY different. He will not remind anybody of Dorian Yates, but he will definitely be a powerhouse.

Just think about it. You do not expect a just-planted seed to grow in 3 hours, right? So do not expect your strength and muscles to grow that fast. It is a daily routine. The only method to speed up results is to find what works for you, and stick to it for as many days per year as possible.

Patience always pays off.

Closing Thoughts

Strength and physique building is not rocket science. Yes, it involves thinking, but everything is plain and simple (not easy, though). I hope this article taught you something new. Follow these principles and get the results you deserved.

ROUGH STRENGTH BASICS: HOW TO GAIN STRENGTH?

The majority of people that are interested in strength training are concerned with the wrong things. They think too much about exercise machines, biceps curls, what training gloves to use, which is better - barbells or dumbbells, when to train - in the morning or in the evening, or maybe in the afternoon? What to eat pre-workout, intra-workout and post-workout, 'anabolic windows', what split to use, what supplements to use, or should I train biceps with triceps or separately? Holy crap, these questions make me want to puke in the mouth of the person who asks them. *The best thing you can do to your training is to concentrate on BASICS and forget everything else for 3-5 years straight.*

But les us get back to the theme.

What Is Strength?

Zatsiorsky, who is constantly quoted by strength coaches, defines strength as the ability to overcome or counteract external resistance through muscular action (Zatsiorsky, 1995). I totally agree with such a definition. However, I want to add that strength can be different. For example, explosive strength and maximal strength are not the same things despite the common word. Typically, strength can be divided into five categories: absolute strength, maximal strength, explosive strength, speed strength, and strength endurance. Here is a quick overview of these different categories:

Absolute strength is the amount of force that one can exert under involuntary muscle stimulation (ex. electrical stimulation).

Maximal Strength is the amount of force that one can exert under voluntary effort.

Explosive Strength is the ability to express significant tension in minimal time.

Speed Strength is the ability to quickly execute an unloaded movement or a movement against a relatively small external resistance.

Strength Endurance is the ability to effectively maintain muscular function under work conditions of long duration.

All of the above definitions are taken from Ross Enamait's awesome book on bodyweight training "Never Gymless". Check it out.

The important take-home point here is that strength is not just strength. There are several types of it and they differ significantly. You can develop all of them with proper training. They require different approaches, but the main principle remains the same - the biggest secret in how to gain strength. You will not believe it, but it is progressive resistance.

How to Gain Strength?

When we are talking about pure strength, nervous system training should be our primary concern. Our strength is determined by the speed of CNS signals from the brain to nerve endings. A better path for neurons means more strength, in layman terms. So the main question we should ask ourselves (if our goal is to gain strength) is how to improve our neural pathways? Well, the best answer I learnt was to perform the skill as often as possible, while staying as fresh as possible. I used word "skill" with a purpose. Strength is a skill. Just like playing guitar, or drawing, or riding a bicycle. The more you practice the better you get at it. The same is true for strength, although it is not that obvious. Therefore, if you want to gain strength you need frequent repetition of the skill. So all you need is to Squat and Deadlift heavy every day or even several times per day, right? Not quite. While sometimes it may be a viable option for professional athletes, it will be overkill for regular fitness enthusiasts whose goal is just to get strong, not to set world records. There is so-called volume/intensity/frequency mix (we will talk a bit later about it). If you increase one of the variables, then you should decrease other two. So how should you use this awesome information above?

Routines for Strength

In my experience, the best routines for strength are moderate-frequency low-volume and low-repetition ones. Why low rep? Because it is a rule. Repetitions from 1 to 5 build strength (and muscle in some cases) because they use specific energy stores and specific muscle fibers. Low volume will allow you to train more frequently. What about intensity? It should be kept high. I would say at least 75-80% of your 1 rep max. Remember: "Train, don't strain!" Too much intensity will lead to less frequency, which is unwanted. Here is couple of example routines for strength:

Example Routine #1 (Starting Strength Variation)

Day 1
1) Sandbag Zercher Squats 3 x 5
2) Double Kettlebell Military Press 3 x 5
3) Weighted Pull-Ups 3 x 5

Day 2 - Off

Day 3
1) Sandbag Zercher Squats 3 x 5
2) One-Arm Push-Up Progression 3 x 5
3) Sandbag Shouldering 3 x 5

Day 4 - Off

Day 5
1) Sandbag Zercher Squats 3 x 5
2) Bulgarian Ring Dips 3 x 5
3) Kettlebell Renegade Row 3 x 5

Day 6 & 7 - Off

Day 8 - Repeat

Example Routine #2 (Power to the People Variation)

Day 1-5
1) Planche Push-Ups Progression 2 x 5
2) Double Sandbag Deadlift 2 x 5

Day 6 & 7 - Off

Day 8 - Repeat

Note: of course, these routines are just examples. If you want to use them, you will need to scale the intensity to your current strength levels.

What to do if you want to develop other kinds of strength? Well, it all depends on what qualities you want to develop, and how long does it take to recuperate from one training session to another. You can add 1-2 additional training sessions per week where you will train Explosive Push-Ups and One-Arm Kettlebell Snatches for 5-8 sets of 3 with as much explosiveness as possible. Or you can add some speed work in some lifts, for example, Barbell Squats with resistance bands. The set/rep protocol remains the same. You get the idea. The more different kinds of strength you want to train, the less your total weekly volume per one type of strength should be.

What Training Implement Is the Best for Building Strength?

Obviously, there is no best tool to develop strength. All of them have their advantages and disadvantages. Of course, ultimate results in strength require mixing training implements. However, it is better to be good in one thing than just play with several. If you like bodyweight strength training, then why not get strong with it? You should do what you like. If you prefer lifting barbells, then use them. Every training implement has its unique value in training. For example, you will have a hard time finding a better exercise for leg strength and size than Barbell Squats. There is no analogue to strength built by manipulating your bodyweight on still rings. Sandbag training has its own benefits. Awareness of these pluses and minuses can lead to ultimate mix of implements for you.

Closing Thoughts

Get strong. Everything else will follow. Strength should be anyone's number one priority. It is not well known, but strength built in the gym carries over to other areas in life: career, relationships, etc. The stronger you are, the more confidence you have, and the more mental strength you possess. It is definitely worth the time. Get strong. Now you have all the information you need.

ROUGH STRENGTH BASICS: HOW TO BUILD MUSCLE?

So in addition to strength, you want to build some muscle. Luckily, this information will help you with your goal.

What Is Muscle Building?

Muscle building or, as geeks say, hypertrophy, is an increase in the size of a muscle through an increase in the size of its component cells. It occurs due to the principle of supercompensation. This principle states that a muscle increases its size as a reaction to stress and microtrauma induced by exercise. In simpler words, when we exercise, we totally blast our muscles, the body thinks "what the fuck? I better be bigger next time this asshole will torture me like that" and grows.

There are several stages of muscle building process: microtrauma, compensation and supercompensation.

- microtrauma – exercise period, the time when we train our muscles;
- compensation - recovery period, the time when our muscles return to their original size;
- supercompensation - growth period, the time when our muscles increase their size.

Look at the Training Effect/Recovery chart on the next page (the concept introduced by the Hungarian scientist N. Yakovlev):

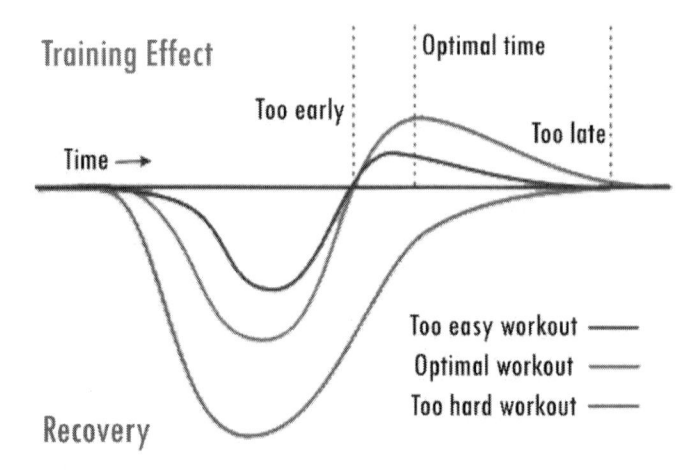

As you can see, horizontally we have time, vertically – microtrauma in the bottom and supercompensation at the top. Middle line is our base level. The first workout line from the top is the training effect from a too easy workout, the last is from too hard, and the middle is the sweet spot. Depending on intensity, volume and frequency, we can get a different training effect. When intensity and volume are too high, we get a "too hard workout". When they are too little – a "too easy" one. Regarding frequency, you can find the "Too early", "Optimal time" and "Too late" markers. If frequency is too high for a given intensity and volume, we will be at the "too early" marker. If it is too low, then at the "too late" one. "Optimal time" is the sweet spot where we get the most gains.

Bla, bla, bla, enough of this nerdy scientific stuff. Who cares about it anyway? Let us get to the important information.

How to Build Muscle?
To build muscle, you need to follow several basic guidelines:
- make your resistance progressive;
- your program should contain enough training volume;
- be in caloric surplus;
- eat enough protein.

Make your resistance progressive. Firstly, progressive resistance is the main recipe for success. You need to get stronger to grow. If you bench 50 kg all your life, you will be looking exactly like that. On the other hand, you will definitely grow if you bench press 100 kg, and then 120, and then 140 with enough volume. You will never grow if you do just regular Push-Ups. However, you will have the opportunity to get bigger if you progress to Planche Push-ups or strict One-Arm Push-Ups, or harder variations like Ring Dips. Increasing intensity is not the only way to make resistance progressive, however, most of the time it is the most beneficial.

Secondly, you need to progress in BASIC exercises. For those who are not familiar with them, these are the ones that involve more than one joint. They are the various presses, rows, squats and pulls. Why do you need to bother with them? Because they involve much more musculature than isolation exercises. I am not saying here that isolation exercises (the ones that involve one joint) are useless. They have their own aim (for example, to fix muscle imbalances). Still they fall short compared to multi-joint exercises in the case of muscle building. If you see a big (and especially lean) natural guy training, then he's probably pretty strong in basic exercises (as experience shows). That is why strength is so important.

So you got it: progressive resistance + basic exercises.

Your program should contain enough training volume. Low volume programs are awesome to some point. However, there are two situations with them after the initial gains:

1. You still progress and grow.
2. You still progress, but do not grow.

In the second case, all you need to do is to increase the training volume. In addition, you need to switch training programs from time to time. And sometimes (when you have a solid strength base and at least one year of uninterrupted training under your belt) you need to switch from moderate to high volume programs to shake things up and to grow more. According to experts, you need approximately 25 reps total per movement to make strength and size gains. Sometimes you will need to go up to 50 reps total (of course, no strength gains, just size). As for rep range, many coaches prescribe 6-12 reps per set. Does this mean that 1-5 rep range does not build muscle? No, it does, but with low reps, oftentimes you will need to perform more sets.

Be in caloric surplus. If you want to build muscle, then you need to eat. It is a no-brainer. However, the important thing is that you can build muscle only at a really slow pace. Therefore, do not rush it. You cannot get 21-inch guns overnight. If you rush progress, you will only get fat, and nobody except you will know that there are muscles under that fat. Decent muscles are built over years, and even decades for some people. I would recommend minimizing fat gain as much as possible. If you have moderate-to-slow metabolism, do not be a fool, and add only 200-300 calories to your daily number (more on this in "Nutrition" section). If you gain 0.5 kg per month, it is awesome progress, and it is probably all muscle. Watch your waist. It should not change if you are lean.

Eat enough protein. Protein is very tricky topic. Some people say you need just 1 g per 1 lb, and that works for them. Others say you need 1.5 to 2 g per 1 lb and that is working for them. So where is the truth? Well, I would rather eat more protein than less. You do not want to hamper your muscle building process by not eating enough of the most useful macronutrient, right? If you grow on low and moderate protein quantities and that all is muscle, not fat - good for you. You are a lucky bastard. Yet I know that the more protein I eat the better I look and perform. And I do not mean that you need to use supplements. Not at all. You can get it all from whole foods.

Example Routine for Muscle Building

I used Iron Addict's SPBR with a lot of success with me and my clients. This template is great. Here is a variation you can use to build muscle:

Monday
1) Sandbag Push-Press 3 x 5
2) Dumbbell Incline Bench Press 4 x 8
3) Kettlebell One-Arm Seated Press 3 x 8 (each arm)
4) Bodyweight Triceps Extensions 3 x 12

Wednesday
1) Single-Leg Squats 3 x 5
2) Weighted Chin-Ups 4 x 6
3) Sandbag Bear Hug Good Mornings 2 x 10
4) Rings Bodyweight Curls 3 x 10

Friday
1) Weighted Dips 3 x 5
2) Kettlebell Floor Press 4 x 8
3) Wall-Assisted Handstand Push-Ups 3 x 8
4) Rings Triceps Extensions 3 x 10

Monday
1) Double Kettlebell Swings 3 x 3
2) Sandbag Shoulder Squats 2 x 10 (1 for each side)
3) Front Lever Rows 4 x 6
4) Sandbag Biceps Curls 3 x 12

Wednesday
Start over with 'Monday'.

Note: of course, you will need to scale the intensity to your current levels. That is just the basic template.

Closing Thoughts

So these are the basics of muscle building. Now you have the information and a sample routine. It is time to implement this stuff into practice.

VOLUME/INTENSITY/FREQUENCY RELATIONSHIP IN STRENGTH TRAINING

Volume, intensity, and frequency: these are the basics of proper programming in strength training. Obviously, if your program does not deliver results you expect, then you screwed up one of these three. Of course, this is assuming that you already made training resistance progressively harder over time. It seems that people nowadays have no idea how to find the right and, most importantly, proper balance between volume, intensity and frequency. So if these three strength-training variables are so important, then how can you mix them correctly? This article will explain how. However, at first you will need a brief overview of what volume, intensity and frequency are.

Training Volume

In a couple of words, training volume is the amount of work done. It can be measured in different ways. For example, training volume can be estimated in total reps per exercise, in the total amount of sets per training session, in the total amount of weight lifted in exercise per training session, in the total amount of sets or reps per day or per week, or per year etc. Proper training volume is regulated by the recovery ability of the person and his/her goal. If your goal is pure strength, or sparing strength and muscle during a caloric deficit, then you need less volume. If your goal is to build muscle, then you may need more. Most of the bodybuilding routines nowadays are plain old high-volume training.

Training Intensity

Training intensity, in layman terms, is how hard you train. In other words that are more scientific, it is the percentage of your one repetition maximum [1RM]. The closer your working weight to 1RM - the harder you work, the higher the intensity, the less reps you will be able to perform in set, the more time you will need to fully recover between sets, the less total sets you will be able to perform. Intensity is very important in gaining strength as well as in building muscle, as well as in sparing muscle during a caloric restriction. It should be kept pretty high if your goal is pure strength and/or getting ripped. However, if your goal is building as much muscle as possible you need to lower intensity a bit to allow more volume.

Training Frequency

Training frequency is how often you perform certain moves, practice certain exercises, or train certain muscles. Frequency can be high and low. High frequency means at least 3 times per week, but usually even more. Low frequency is no more than 2 times per week, but usually even less. Well, there is no hard rule on this, but in my opinion, such classification is not far from the truth. Frequency is great for neural adaptation. This means that it is great for building strength and skill. In addition, it is pretty good for building muscle as you get stronger faster while adding more total volume. For fat loss, it's probably not the most important variable.

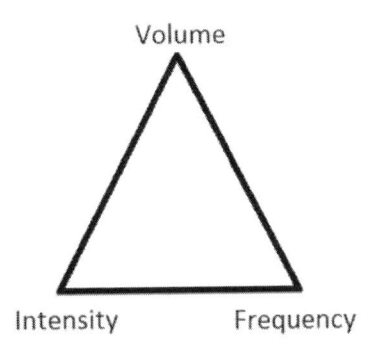

The volume, intensity, and frequency relationship in strength training

How to Mix Them Properly?

As you can see from the picture above, training volume, intensity and frequency are mutually exclusive variables. The more you increase one of them - the less the other two should be. This means that if you increase the volume, then your intensity and frequency should go down for you to be able to progress. As well as when you increase frequency, intensity and volume should go down. You get the idea.

Why is it so? The answer is recovery. To progress you need to recover between training sessions. In other words, if you do not do more reps or sets, or perform harder exercises, or lift heavier weight from session to session (or at least several sessions per month if you are at intermediate level), then you are probably not recovering between them. In this case, you need to decrease one of the variables (or all of them) and see how you doing. You will probably need to do this until you find the right amount of each variable individually for you. *One tip: if you need to lower one of these training variables, I would go with volume first and intensity and frequency second.*

In my experience, most people progress nicely on low volume high frequency programs. On the other hand, high volume and low frequency, mid intensity programs work with much less success. By the way, the same goes for "deloading". I would rather do fewer reps or fewer sets with heavy weight than deload to the same set-rep scheme with lighter weight. It seems the former actually refreshes you, while the latter makes you weaker. But that is just my experience.

Well, when you have found out what volume/intensity/frequency mix is optimal for you to recover and progress, you can experiment with variables to get different results. You can lower the intensity, increase the volume and frequency, and see what this will do for you. For example, instead of bench pressing once a week, do hundreds of push-ups every day. Or you can increase intensity and lower volume and frequency. For example, instead of squatting moderately 2-3 times a week, do a heavy max effort session once every 10 days and see what this will do for you.

Finally, proper programming is all about finding a "sweet spot" in volume/intensity/frequency mix. How do you know whether you have found it? Easy. You should progress to heavier exercises, lift more weight, do more reps and/or sets etc. That is how.

Closing Thoughts

Strength training programming is not rocket science. It is pretty basic in nature. You need to understand several things and you will be able to reach your goals. And training volume, intensity and frequency are those things. If your program does not work, you should check these training variables out. It is as simple as that.

TRAINING PLAN VS INSTINCTS

"Planning vs instincts" is a quite controversial topic in strength training circles. Some people will say: "Planning your workouts? Are you kidding me? I just come to [insert place where the person usually trains] and just go by feel. Planning is for nerds. Training should be fun". Others will argue: "Planning might not be the most fun thing in the world, but it gives you the chance not to screw up badly with your training and get results (because you always know what to do and what intensity will be adequate). Going by feel is for people that are so stupid, that can't even make a simple plan for themselves". The battle can go on and on and everybody will remain with his/her belief.

Nevertheless, I will share with you my experience with these two types of training.

Instinctive Training

Instinctive training is when you do not plan anything. You just come to gym/park/home gym and do whatever you want to do with hope that you will be stronger/bigger/leaner next time. What is interesting - the fact that this kind of training actually works for some individuals. Of course, laws of effective training are equal for everybody. While those dudes and dudettes might think that they are training according to their instincts, in reality, they are following the same principles as everybody; they just do not know they are.

Surprisingly, many people follow this type of training. In my opinion, most of them are just wasting their time. Yeah, they progress to some point, but sooner rather than later they hit plateau. What happens to this huge majority of trainees for whom instinctive training just does not work? Some of them quit, some of them stay there, thinking that they have reached their genetic potential (that 75 kg bench press is definitely your genetic limit if you are stupid enough to believe that). Some of them start using steroids (how unexpectedly), but the most adequate of them start educating themselves and discover planning.

Planning Your Training

As you can see, I favor planned training much more. There is a reason for this. As experience shows, purely instinctive training works only for guys with great genetics. Other people with average and less (like me) do MUCH better with training plans or programs. With training plans, you have more control about what will happen with your strength and physique as a result. Start with a training log. *I started seeing results from training only after I began writing everything down into my training log.* After that, with years of experimentation, I came up with training techniques that work for me. You should do the same. Start a training log. Pick a program and write everything down. Test-drive it for at least 4 weeks. Then analyze the data and decide whether this approach works for you or not.

So planned training is the best and instinctive training is crap, right? Not so fast.

The Truth

Well, the truth is, as always, in the middle. Both types have their place in training regimens of athletes and regular fitness enthusiasts, at least in different periods of their training careers. Nowadays I use both of them. I cannot go just by feel because I will turn myself into skinny fat weak bastard. I always plan my workouts. However, plans tend to go wrong sometimes. That is when you need to listen to yourself, of course, if you are able to hear what your body says to you.

My final advice would be to plan your training because this way it will be much more predictable. Though never forget to have fun with your workouts.

FULL-BODY ROUTINE OR SPLIT: SO WHAT'S BETTER?

Full-body routine is a program that calls for training your whole body every session.

Split routine allows training just a part of the body per session.

So here is the question: what is better? Are splits more effective, or full-body workouts are superior? Let us analyze and find out.

Pros and Cons of Full-Body Routines and Splits

Main pros of full-body routines:

- *Whole body stimulation*, obviously. The more muscles we stimulate in workout the more effective it should be.

- *Greater frequency of stimulation*. The more we practice, the faster we will get good at something.

- *No "fluff"*. You have limited amount of time, so you choose big compound lifts almost exclusively.

Main cons of full-body routines:

- *Some people just cannot tolerate them*. No matter how you structure everything, some people will not be able to progress on full-body routines.

- *Some body parts will lag in development*. Yes, full-body routines give you freedom from "fluff" exercises, but some body parts will grow faster than others, which shouldn't bother you if your primary goals are strength and performance.

Main pros of splits:

- *Lots of recovery*. You just work some body part to total exhaustion and rest for a week or so.

- *Allow more volume*. You definitely can do more work sets in split routines, which can be better for building muscle.

- *Allow more variety*. This can be important for bodybuilding.

Main cons of splits:

- *Sometimes not enough frequency.* This is especially true for beginners who need more frequent stimulation to progress faster.
- Many people end up *doing ton of isolation exercises instead of compound lifts*. This is totally wrong.

I may have forgotten some things, but it does not matter. The point is that both full-body routines and splits have their own purpose. Implement one or the other in wrong situation and you may not get any training results, or worse, bad ones.

What Does My Experience Show?

There are several cases when splits are actually better than full-body routines. Firstly, it is all about recovery. I always could tolerate full-body routines and progress with them. Well, now I understand why. This is because I always try to sleep at least 8 hours per night; because I eat lots of protein and my diet is right for me; because I rarely give a fuck about things I can't control in any way (this is how you have much less stress in your life). Finally, it is because I do not waste my time on crap and try to live my life fully. But that's just me. You, on the other hand, can have several kids, work two jobs you hate, have a bad relationship, sleep 4 hours per night, eat junk, and despise your life. In this case, full-body routines are not for you. In this case, your only way out is to start a fight club. With all seriousness, if you have suboptimal conditions in life, you may not be able to tolerate full-body routines. I work with many people who have very busy schedules and hard lives. The harder their conditions the less they can tolerate.

Full-body routines are best for beginners. The demands of training are pretty low, and they progress much faster, for example, squatting 3 times per week than just one time. However, with increasing demands of training you might not be able to train your whole body every training session. This is the right time to try splits. If you have done Mon-Wed-Fri full body, try Mon – upper; Tue – lower; Thu – upper; Fri – lower. If that is too much, try Mon – upper; Wed – lower; Fri – upper; Mon – lower.

Splits work. Take me as example. I trained whole body every session for a decent period of time. It worked like a clock. I was able to progress every session. If I was not progressing, I just changed the exercise variation, and everything worked again. However, then came time to use some kind of split. Why? Because the intensity of the exercises got really high. I could not recover from full-body training anymore. Did I get less result with splits comparing to full-body routines? No, training intensity still continued to grow. In addition, take into account that I had no other option, unless I wanted to train two times per week or less. My point here is that splits can be not just a viable option, but also the only option.

Also a note on bodybuilding: in this sport, you will need decent training volume. If you want to keep intensity pretty high, you will need to cut frequency. To quote Dave Tate:

"It boils down to common sense. Look at the bodybuilders winning shows – whether they're pros or amateurs or natural competitors – they all follow a basic template: 2-3 exercises per body part, 3-5 sets of 6-12 reps, each set taken just shy of failure, and each body part trained every 3-7 days.
That's basically what most of them do, so why reinvent the wheel?"

Listen to a wise man.

With Calisthenics Everything Is Trickier

Why? Because in harder exercises you will need to use your whole body, not just chest and triceps, or back and biceps. For example, after Straddle Planche Push-Ups I clearly feel the pump not only in my chest, shoulders and triceps, but also in my biceps, hamstrings, lats, abs and lower back. During One-Arm Push-Ups you should flex quads as much as possible. As a result, it is much harder to program these movements conventionally because when you get to very challenging variations, you should work with your whole body. While, for example, Straddle Planche Push-Up technically is a press, you will feel it not only in chest, shoulders and triceps, but also in other muscles that are usually not associated with presses.

Closing Thoughts

So what is better: full-body routines or splits? As you probably already have figured out, neither is better. Either of them has its own place in the world of training. You may prefer one or another. They both work. If you can tolerate full-body routines, then you should go with them. If not, then use splits. Not crappy splits, but reasonable ones. Do not use a split as an excuse not to squat, concentrate on compound lifts, get stronger in them, and you will get results.

INCREASE YOUR STRENGTH WITH DOUBLE PROGRESSION

So you've been training for some time. Some of it you have wasted because you were following "programs of champions" or other bodybuilding magazines' crap. After realizing that you're not getting anywhere or getting somewhere but not where you want to, you have decided to do it right finally. You have concentrated on training strength, you have made your diet right, and you have finally started to see some progress in working weights as well as body composition. However, after some time everything became harder and gaining strength is not that easy and fast as it was. You started thinking and analyzing…

That is the time when you need more sophisticated approach. Why not make use of good old double progression?

What Is Double Progression?

When you progress just in one training variable (i.e. weight or reps, or sets etc.), it is single progression. Double progression, on the other hand, requires progressing in several parameters. Two, to be clear. You may even implement triple progression and more, but I want to concentrate on one variation of double progression I came up with lately.

Why bother? When you will get to intermediate training stage, you will understand why. You will not be able to progress in weight every training session (if you were able to do that, you would be squatting 500 kg in a year; that will not happen, no matter how hard you try). However, you will be able to progress in other training parameters like reps, sets, rest periods etc. This is where double progression becomes really handy.

How to Implement Double Progression?

There are several ways to implement double progression in your training routine. In easier words, pick two training variables, set the working range and progress in it. For example, you can do 3 sets of 6 reps in Military Press with 50 kg. Work up to 3 sets of 8 reps, then increase the weight to 52.5 kg the next session and start over with 3 sets of 6 reps. Two training variables: weight and reps. Everything else should remain constant. Working range: 6 to 8 reps.

Another example would be Rest-Pause training. Let us assume that you want to improve the Barbell Deadlift. Pick a weight that is your 3RM and do 10 singles with it. Rest periods: 60 s. Work up to 10 singles with 10-second rest periods. Then increase weight and start over. Two training variables: weight and rest periods. Working range: 60 to 10 seconds rest periods.

Rough Strength Double Progression Solution

Of course, somebody has already come up with such method of progression. I am not saying that it is my invention, but who cares anyway (except for geeks and nerds)? The important thing is that this approach works and works very well. So you pick an exercise, say, the Barbell Squat. Pick a weight that is your 5-repetition maximum. Do 5 sets of 3 reps. Return in a week, and do 4 sets of 4. Then again, return after seven days and do 3 sets of 5. Add weight and start over with 5 sets of 3. This way you really master the weight. You work with it for at least 3 training sessions. It may sound too slow, but in fact, it is not. You cannot gain strength much faster than that at intermediate level. It is not going to happen. Besides, the steadier you build your strength, the longer your current type of progression will work. If you for some reason cannot get all the reps in all sets, do not worry and work with this weight until you get all of them.

```
5 x 3
4 x 4
3 x 5
Start over
```

Closing Thoughts

So if you need a strength boost, take a close look at this double progression thing. Maybe it is just the perfect solution you needed to progress further. Slow but steady.

THE MOST FLEXIBLE SET/REPETITION SCHEME EVER

The most flexible set/rep scheme [FSRS] is an unconventional way to organize your workout. Instead of boring 5 sets of 5, or 3 sets of 10, or 8 sets of 3, or 4 sets of 4, or 3 sets of 3, or 4 sets of 12, or 3 sets of 6, or any other X sets of Y, *you count only total number or reps* (the number of sets doesn't really matter as long as you meet your volume requirement (your total)). Just look at traditional templates. Every one of them has a predetermined amount of volume. Multiply sets and reps: 5 x 5 is 25 repetitions in total, 4 x 6 is 24, 3 x 10 is 30, etc. What if you don't really need to organize that volume in set in stone 5 x 5 or 6 x 4? Who said that you need to perform precisely 5 sets of 5 reps to get results? What if you are lifting such a heavy weight (or performing such a hard exercise) that you can't finish 5 reps on all the 5 sets for a whole month (or several months) of regular attempts? Well, FSRS is definitely a solution to these problems.

How Does It Work?

You choose the exercise, abandon all your dreams and expectations of using conventional set/rep template and pick the desired amount of repetitions. How to choose it? Generally, the less reps you choose, the more it will be strength-targeted work; more volume, the more hypertrophy-oriented it is. I would say that 9-25 reps would be "strength", while 25-50 would be "muscle" with 25 as a "sweet spot". Are <9 and >50 totals useless? No. They have their own place in training world, but they should be used only if you clearly understand what you are doing. For example, with advanced calisthenics stuff, you might not be able to finish 9 reps total, but you won't have any other option as it is the progression step you need to master and there is no way around. That is when <9 total is appropriate. Regarding going over 50, it is endurance work. Use that amount of reps only if your goal is to be able to perform a given exercise for longer periods of time.

You have picked the total volume, so what is next? Now you need to decide what this exercise is for. If it is the main strength move, then your intensity should be higher. If it is hypertrophy/assistance exercise, then the intensity should be lower. How to measure intensity? It will be determined by the amount of reps you can perform on the first set. In other words, we will use the repetition maximum concept. If your goal is strength, your intensity should not exceed your 6-8 repetition maximum [RM]. It means that you should pick such a weight (exercise) that you will not be able to complete 9 reps with (in). If you can, then it is hypertrophy/assistance work.

So let us assume you have picked Planche Push-Ups. You want to do 25 reps total. It is strength work, and you cannot do more than 7 reps in the first set. It is your 7RM. Your workout can look like this:

Set 1 – 6 reps (one rep in the tank)
Set 2 – 6 reps (you are pretty strong)
Set 3 – 5 reps (fatigue kicks in)
Set 4 – 3 reps
Set 5 – 3 reps
Set 6 – 2 reps (finally finished)
Total: 25 reps

Let us have another example. Now it will be muscle-building work. Let us say it is the Double Kettlebell Military Press. You need to perform 30 reps total, and 32 kg is your 10RM. Your workout may look like this:

Set 1 – 9 reps (still in the tank, baby)
Set 2 – 8 reps
Set 3 – 7 reps
Set 4 – 6 reps (done)
Total: 30 reps

As you can see, there is nothing hard with this FSRS thing, but this leads to another question…

How to Progress with FSRS?

Easier than you think. There are several ways to move forward with it:

- *Weight/intensity progression.* It is the most obvious way. If you use, say, 6RM weight/exercise and progressed to 7-8 reps in first set then it is time to move on and add resistance. NOTICE: this may not be true for purely advanced calisthenics work. You may need to wait and get stronger to move forward.

- *Rep progression.* Let us take the previous 6RM example. Assuming you are performing a 20 rep total, your workout can look like this: 5, 4, 4, 3, 2, 2. Instead of trying to perform more reps in the first set, which can be impossible sometimes, you can add reps to the next ones. The following workout can be something along the lines of 5, 5, 4, 4, 2.

- *Set progression.* As you can see in the example above, second workout was performed in less sets than the first one. This is the set progression of FSRS.

- *Rest progression.* Use shorter rest period between sets. It is that simple.

I may have forgotten some things, but this will keep you busy for some time.

What is with Static Holds?

Everything is absolutely the same, but instead of reps you have seconds. That "sweet spot" of 25 total repetitions equals approximately 60 total seconds. Some people tend to increase this number, some – decrease. My math uses the following logic (it is only my experience, it can vary for different people): a 15 seconds hold equals roughly 6 repetitions according to feeling and fatigue; 24 = 6 reps x 4 sets. 15 sec x 4 sets = 60 sec. It is not science though.

How to Alternate Sets Properly with FSRS?

With FSRS, you can face a little problem. I will show you an example. Let us assume that you want to use FSRS with two exercises. In addition, you want to alternate between them to compress your workout and have more time to hang out with friends, drink alcohol, and get the worst hangover the next morning. While performing sets, you find out with terror that you have hit your total in exercise #1 while exercise #2 requires another set. What to do? Rest and do the damn set.

How Did I Find Out About It?

Minute of history. Of course, this template is far from new, as is almost everything in strength training nowadays. I was introduced to this concept by articles of Chad Waterbury. I do not know whether he was the first one, but after his article lots of trainers started implementing FSRS with success. I personally use it a lot if not in every exercise. *It became so essential for my training that I cannot imagine working out without FSRS.*

The problem with conventional set/rep templates is that they are too fixed. People in the weight training world are constantly having this problem of the inability to finish the given amount of reps in every set. Just like this: you do 5, 5, 5 with happy thought that you'll finally crush it this week, but then do something like 3, 3. What the fuck? If you experienced such situation, know that you are not alone. Most of the trainees have the same problem. That is exactly why such schemes as 12-10-8-6 and FSRS were born. In addition, set-in-stone templates like 3 x 10 or 4 x 8 (I intentionally used high reps) almost never work for calisthenics. With bodyweight training, you have to be creative because of the decent jumps in intensity. You cannot just do 5 x 5 and add 2.5 kg (well, you can, but more on this later).

Closing Thoughts

In conclusion, I would like to say just one thing. If you are tired of those traditional set/rep schemes or you have unstoppable urge to use something ultra-flexible, then I encourage you to try FSRS. It is simple and incredible. Do you really need anything more?

TOOLS: CALISTHENICS

CALISTHENICS OR WEIGHT TRAINING – WHICH ONE IS BETTER?

Bodyweight or weight training? A lot of people get confused about their choice. They try to find the ultimate tool for gaining strength, building muscle, and getting ripped. Some of them become fans of one tool, some prefer the other one. However, often it does not stop there. Some of them just need to make their point of view the only possibility. And there is no better place to argue it than the internet. That is why we have epic battles of calisthenics disciples and weight training advocates. Life-or-death battles. The result is that we get even more confused.

As an open-minded, reasonable, and smart trainee, you should ask yourself: "Ok, so which one is better?" The answer may surprise you.

So Which One Is Better?

The right answer is neither. Neither is better. Calisthenics as well as weight training have their own places in the world of training. Well, I may go even further and state this: it is possible that you will not get complete development with just one of them. Besides, you can always mix them as you wish. One does not exclude the other. Old time strongmen knew this. Their goal was ultimate strength. They did not divide their strength training into tools like we see now. If they could not move their body through space, then they were weak and worked on that area. If they could not lift the barbell, dumbbell, or kettlebell in the way they wanted, then they were weak and worked on that area of strength. If they could not lift sandbags, stones or other real-world objects, they considered themselves weak and worked on that area. I like this approach. This way you have no weak links. Listen to old school wisdom. Do not be afraid to cheat on your favorite training tool with the other. It is not cheating – it is all-around strength development. Do not limit yourself to one implement. They all are fun and useful.

But How Can I Get Time for All of Them?

Well, try to find it. Again, you do not need to devote a lot of time and effort to minor tools. For example, if your main priority is bodyweight proficiency, then you can add 2-4 training sessions per week with weights. Use a simple approach like Pavel's "3-5 method". You can learn it from his book "Beyond Bodybuilding". If your main goal is to master weights, it would be by all means wise and beneficial idea to throw in some dips, pull-ups, pistols and handstands to the mix.

Closing Thoughts

It is really frustrating when people start to idealize one tool over another. As experience shows, there is no such thing as "the ultimate training implement". All of them have their pros and cons, as well as different practical application.

If your goal is to build as much muscle as possible and you do not care about strength (I do not get it, but there are lots of such people out there), then weights are your best friends. There is no point in bothering with calisthenics.

If your goal is to be able to control your body, then there is no crucial point in using weights.

However, if you crave greater strength, then I suggest you to combine weights and calisthenics to get more from your training.

ARE CALISTHENICS OPTIMAL FOR BUILDING MUSCLE?

Bodyweight strength training was a revelation for me. I was quite ignorant for some time, and thought that weight training is a must if your goal is to gain strength and build muscle. When I was introduced to progressive calisthenics, my world was turned upside down. It was a golden gem. Now I have solid experience with this kind of training and here is the question I want to discuss: is bodyweight strength training optimal for building muscle?

Why Even Bother?
Well, the benefits of calisthenics are huge:
- No gym memberships
- Almost no equipment
- You can train anytime anywhere
- No restrictions and limits
- Calisthenics provide opportunity for creativity
- You can make almost any movement pattern extremely hard and intense
- It's fun
- They give you the opportunity to learn control over your body.

These are just first things that come to my mind. For me, bodyweight strength training provides one HUGE benefit that blows away any other training implement with ease. It is *sustainability*. Just imagine (well, super hypothetically), the apocalypse came and there are no gyms or weights left on Earth for some reason. How would you train? The answer is calisthenics.

Progressive calisthenics give you a lifetime of opportunity to train and get stronger. You will depend on nothing but your bodyweight and your determination. That is awesome. I like minimalism, and this is minimalism at its finest. It does not matter whether you move to another city or another country, whether you have money for gym membership or weights. Nothing matters except your determination and discipline.

It's All Cool But Back to the Theme, Please

Ok. Are calisthenics optimal for building muscle? Notice how I emphasize the "optimal" aspect. Some may disagree, but *pure calisthenics are not optimal for building muscle*. By "pure" I mean using strictly bodyweight, no weighted vests or chains, etc. Let me explain my point of view.

The thing is that when you use just your bodyweight you depend on progressions. Progressions divide your path in learning given exercise from the easiest step to the hardest. The best progression is the one that has more steps, so the exercise is learned in more gradual manner. Now, for example, compare Barbell Bench Press (BBP) to Planche Push-Up (PPU). In BBP you can start with an empty bar (which is 20 kg), hardly difficult task for anyone except maybe some weak girls. In PPU you start with Pseudo-Planche Push-Ups, these require decent regular Push-Ups and are hard if executed properly. Then in BBP, you can add 2.5 kg to bar, an increment so small that at certain stages you will not even notice it. In PPU, you progress from one position to another and there are great chances that, while you became pretty proficient with current position, you can't even hold the next one. In BBP, you learn proper exercise form right away and then just polish your technique, while adding weight to the bar. In PPU, you learn new exercise every time you move to harder progression step. I think you got the idea.

Barbell with its small increments is the king for building muscle. I guess, it will remain undefeated forever. However, does that mean that calisthenics are waste of time? No. Here is why.

I have used word 'optimal' for a reason. Is bodyweight strength training optimal for building muscle? No. Is it possible to build muscle with it? Hell yes. If your goal is only to build muscle and as fast as possible, then calisthenics are probably not for you. Use barbell or any other training implement that allows you to add resistance gradually. For example, sandbag. But those of you, my friends, who think outside of the box, who are not obsessed with their appearance and want to become super strong with their own body, are welcome to try bodyweight strength training and get awesome body like a byproduct of proper training and nutrition. Though it will require serious dedication.

For Those Who Dare

Firstly, do not forget about progressive resistance and volume. Make your exercise progressively harder over time. Get stronger. If you feel that basic strength training is not enough for growth, add assistance exercises to increase training volume. For example, your upper-body training day can look like this:

Main lift:
1) Strict One-Arm Push-Up 5 x 3

Assistance Work:
A1) Bulgarian Ring Dips 4 x 6-8
A2) Back Lever Pull-Outs 4 x 4-6
B1) Ring Dips 3 x 8-12
B2) Inverted Ring Pull-Ups 3 x 8-12

That is an example for pretty strong dudes, but you get the idea.

Secondly, building muscle is not only about training but also about nutrition. Get a good diet with decent amount of calories and protein. Remember, if you want to build muscle, you need to be in a caloric surplus. If you do not execute this requirement, it does not matter whether you train with a barbell or with bodyweight, you will not build muscle. Also remember that muscle is built slowly, so do not rush the process or you will get fat.

Closing Thoughts

Yes, bodyweight strength training is not the fastest way to build muscle, but remember 'sustainability'? If you got all your muscle with barbell training, that is great, but you will need to train like that forever to sustain it. This means that you will need either your own weights or gym memberships. Calisthenics set you free from this. A body built with calisthenics will be sustainable until your grey hairs. However, if you are a cheap bastard that wants just looks, and fast, then you probably should not dedicate yourself to calisthenics.

HOW TO PROGRESS EFFECTIVELY IN BODYWEIGHT EXERCISES

So you are serious about this calisthenics thing. You have seen lots of videos on YouTube. You have read some articles. Maybe you even have read some books (!). Yet nothing helps. YouTube guys are mostly lightweight, articles are rarely well-written, and books often lack proper guidance because the programming is bad or progression steps are too wide from each other. Most importantly, **they do not teach you how to progress in bodyweight exercises effectively**.

Well, this article should help you then.

Principles of Progression

There are several principles of progression you need to understand. Basically, any skill can be learned knowing them, but I want to emphasize all the attention on calisthenics. So what are those principles?

- Deconstruction
- Progressive Resistance
- Consistency

Different people will put different categories here, but I would like to go with these three.

Deconstruction

I would say it is essential to use deconstruction principle if your goal is to learn any skill. It is all about taking a skill and exploring it from the end result to beginning. If you take the Planche as an example, how can deconstruction can help you?

Let us explore this classic picture of the Planche. What can you tell just from one picture using deconstruction analysis (of course, if you are attentive enough (and have some experience in bodyweight strength training))? Let us start from the toes and move up to the head.

1. The feet are pointing away with toes. Will it help with holding a Planche? Probably not much, but it will make your Planche more aesthetically pleasing.

2. The body is in a perfectly straight line. This is big. You definitely saw all those crappy *NOT-Planches* on YouTube or elsewhere where performer arches his lower back like mad to compensate the lack of strength in his girly weak body. It is wrong and cannot be compared to the true Planche you see in the picture above.

To keep your body in proper line, you will need to practice the Hollow Body Position (just Google it) and to strengthen your core muscles.

A quick note on strengthening core muscles: I have no problem in holding my body straight like in the picture above (my weak link is always shoulders). I can do it because of lots of heavy Squats, Deadlifts, Kettlebell Swings and Snatches, Sandbag Squats and Shoulderings (not Crunches, Sit-Ups and Hyperextentions). If you do not want to add weights to your training regimen, you might lose some awesome lower back development. In this case, concentrate on Hollow Body Position practice, Handstands, Bridges and Back Levers. These would probably be the best options.

3. Shoulders are pushed all the way to the front. This should feel like you are trying flex your trap muscles. Here are two photos to explain what I mean:

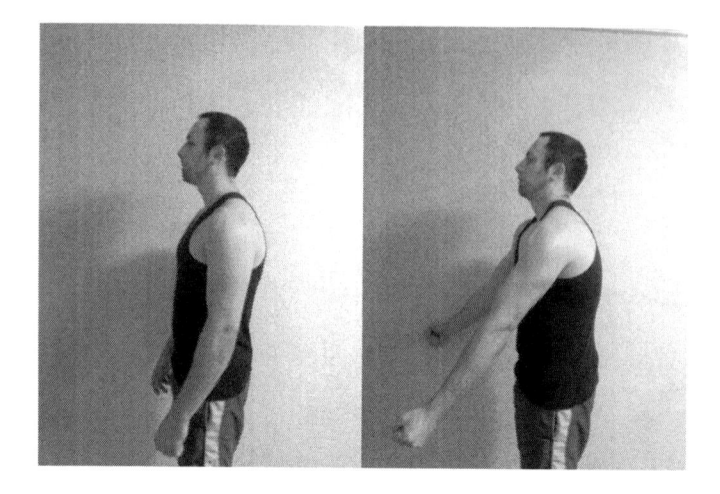

The second one is a proper way to do the Planche, and it will help with your progress big time.

4. The arms are straight. No bent elbows allowed. If you do not lock your elbows, it is not a Planche. Holding this position with fully straight arms is much harder, thus much more beneficial.

5. Hand placement. As you can see, the performer on our photo points his palms forward and due to his lack of flexibility (which is the issue for the majority of the Earth population) he stands more on his fingers rather than on the full palm. The dude can afford to perform Planche like this due to his "lightweightness". But for the heavier guys this would be too close to wrist injury. The simple trick to avoid this is to put your hands pointing a bit to the side. Left hand will point to 10 o'clock and right to 2 o'clock.

Also, notice that the hands are just under the center of gravity of the performer. So this defines Planche as a hand balancing skill. It is similar to the handstand in terms of finding the spot of equilibrium. The most efficient Planche position is the one where hands are placed right under the center of gravity.

6. He looks forward. I think that this position of the head is more beneficial than neutral.

So this was a simple and effective deconstruction analysis of the Planche. You can, and should, do this with any skill you would like to learn. Be as attentive as possible. Even the smallest detail can make a big difference.

Progressive Resistance

I cannot emphasize enough on how this principle is important in strength training, as well as in any area of life. What is progressive resistance (or progressive overload, or whatever you call it)? It's that magic tool that helps you do the impossible. It is that missing part of the puzzle.

Progressive resistance is the principle of breaking down a hard task into several manageable parts (progression steps), and sequencing them in the right order from easiest to the hardest (do you count how many definitions of progressive resistance I give you throughout the book?).

After the deconstruction analysis, you take the skill and break it down into progression steps. It may be not so simple, but with practice, you will become more proficient in this. Let us get back to our Planche example. What is important in mastering the Planche skill? Just looking at the picture you can say that it is important to have the necessary specific strength in shoulders and core, which is pretty close to the truth. You may notice if you are attentive enough that a proper Planche is like an arc.

It should feel like this. Like a bow. You should also notice the lean forward. The Planche is all about leaning forward. Of course, I need to mention that the Planche involves to a great degree your biceps, lats, and upper chest. So what is next? Everything else is common knowledge and common sense. You should probably know by now that the more leverage you have, the easier the position of the exercise. So what is our solution? Increase the leverage and decrease the difficulty.

Here are pretty decent progression steps to the Planche – [2].

To learn the Planche, you need to start with the easiest variation (Planche Lean), and progress through steps to the hardest (Full Planche). Basically, I would recommend such steps:

1. Planche Lean (Get into Push-Up position, lean forward into Pseudo-Planche (your feet should stay on the floor))

2. L-Sit (This position will help to strengthen your arms to hold your bodyweight, and also it will strengthen your core)

3. Tuck Planche (Lean forward into a Planche, but with legs tucked and knees touching your chest)

4. Advanced Tuck Planche (The same as above, but straighten your lower back)

5. Advanced Tuck Planche with the knees outside the elbows (The same

as above, except the position of the legs)

6. Straddle Planche (Lean more forward, keep your body straight, spread your legs apart)

7. Full Planche (Same as above, feet together)

Here you have the basic plan for getting that Planche. Of course, everything may vary from individual to individual. Some people prefer to include One-Leg Planches, Frog Stands, etc., and I am ok with that. What you need to understand is that this progression is not written in stone. *If you find it difficult to progress from one step to the next, the best advice I can give you is to break it further down into several steps.* For example, if you find it difficult to progress from Advanced Tuck to Straddle, take as many steps as needed. The Advanced Tuck Planche with knees outside the elbows is what helped me. Try One-Leg, or try to extend your knees a little more from Advanced Tuck. Again, break it down as many times as needed and pay attention to your weak areas.

Another way to use the progressive resistance principle in learning particularly Planche would be *weighted practice*. If you cannot progress from one step to the next, you can add weight for resistance (more on this in the next article).

And the third way would be *practicing the Planche position with dumbbells*. It is not so fun and much harder to do right, but the potential of smaller weight increments and smaller jumps through progression is worth mentioning. So what you do is take two dumbbells, lie on the bench, press them up, then lower them on straight hands until they reach your center of gravity and pretend you are in Planche position.

Something like this – [3].

Of course, like in any other skill, practicing the actual Planche would be the most beneficial way to train for it. Nevertheless, the other two ways would be a nice accessory means of development. You will need to explore the position some more to find out your weak areas that will need improvement through accessory work.

There are two more points I need to explain in regards to the progressive resistance principle section. The first one is *when to progress?* The good rule of thumb is to progress further when you have mastered the current skill and it feels easy. I know that sounds a bit vague, but in reality everybody will have different numbers. Some people will be able to hold the position for 10 seconds and progress further, while others may need to hold it for 30. Remember that you must not be in hurry or you will fail.

The second one is mixed with the deconstruction stage a bit, and it is *"what will be effective?"* If you feel that you are not progressing, and data proves that what you are doing brings no results, then search for another way. If you do 5 Planche exercises for 5 sets and are not progressing, maybe you need to do less volume and use more intensity. If you do some accessory exercises and they do not give you the boost in performance you are looking for, then maybe you are concentrating on the wrong areas.

Make the resistance progressive and you will be pretty damn close to your goal.

Consistency

Good old hard work. They say that to get good at something you need 10,000 hours of practice. And they are right. Additionally, you will need not just some practice, but reasonable and effective practice. Patience and consistency - that is what will bring you results. Many people overlook this principle, but in reality, that is where most of them fail. You can have a pretty good understanding of the skill, you can have the best progression, but without the hours of practice it is all just theory. What will you do when your workout sucks? What will you do when you hit a plateau? Will you quit? If yes, then you will probably fail at everything in life. Be prepared for hard and long work in learning any skill.

Methods of Progressing in Bodyweight Exercises

So now you know the main principles of learning. Let us get back to calisthenics. Aside from *decreasing leverage*, which was discussed earlier in the example of the Planche, there are several other methods of progressing.

Increasing the range of motion is another effective strategy in learning calisthenics. What is it? Let us take Handstand Push-Ups [HSPU] for example. If you cannot do full range HSPU at the moment, you can decrease the range of motion of the exercise. You can do this with several uninteresting books. Just stack them under your head. Once you hit the desired number of reps, you can just take away one book, work your reps up again and repeat. When you achieve the skill, you can add difficulty with an increased range of motion. In the case of HSPU, once you can do the desired number of reps in the regular version, you can put books or blocks under your hands to increase the range of motion and difficulty at the same time. This method works well with pushing exercises, but is pretty hard to be normally applied to pulling exercises.

Adding weight was discussed earlier, and it is another legitimate way to progress from one progression step to the next. How does it work? Again, let us take the Planche as an example. Let us assume that you can hold an Advanced Tuck version for 15 seconds, but you really struggle to add time because it feels more like training endurance rather than strength. Simultaneously you cannot move to the Straddle version due to lack of strength. No big deal. Try to add weight and stay in this 15 seconds range until you can perform a bodyweight Straddle Planche.

Changing the position of body in space is also very effective way to progress in bodyweight exercises. For example, take One-Arm Push-Up [OAPU]. Let us assume you cannot do single rep in OAPU on the floor. Try to do it off the couch or a curtain pad, or the wall, or anything that works for you. Again, once you hit your desired number of repetitions, progress to lower surfaces until you do it on the floor. The perfect surface for this is power rack with lots of pins. It allows more gradual progression, which is extremely important in OAPU training. And, of course, I mean a real OAPU: feet close, body almost straight, shoulders parallel to the ground.

Combining difficult and easier exercises. I used this method with lots of success for Planche Push-Ups. Just like Ido Portal shows here – [4].

How to use this? Negative and bent-arm parts of the movement will always be stronger than positive and straight-arm parts. So while leaving positive and straight-arm portions of the movement as is, you can easily make negative and bent-arm portions harder.

For example, you can do Planche Push-Ups with different progression steps at the top and bottom. Start with Tuck Planche and while lowering down spread the legs into a bottom Straddle Planche. Tuck the legs back at the top.

Or if you train with a partner, you can try additionally increase difficulty of the negative part with added weight, while removing it from the positive part. For example, the partner can put a sandbag on your back in the Push-Up. At the bottom, he will just remove it and you will push back up without a bag.

Combining exercises into more complex moves. Adding weight or increasing the range of motion are not the only methods in your arsenal. Try combining exercises. For example, if you became proficient in Muscle-Ups and Front Levers, you can combine them into a Muscle-Up to Front Lever sequence and perform them like one exercise. This is freedom. No boundaries.

Closing Thoughts

So now you have the basic knowledge on attaining any skill and progressing in bodyweight exercises. Use this knowledge wisely. Apply it and let me know how it worked.

WEIGHTED CALISTHENICS: THE BEST OF BOTH WORLDS

In this article, we will explore ways of utilizing external weights to make calisthenics more challenging and interesting. In addition, you will learn how to make bodyweight strength progressions easier. Let's go.

How Did I Discover Weighted Calisthenics?

You might think: "Are you retarded or what? Every bonehead gym rat knows that you can add weight to bodyweight exercises to make them harder". Well, I knew that as well. Additionally, I knew that weighted vests are awesome training tools. The problem is that they cost a lot. If you can afford them - cool, buy one without even thinking, if you are into this calisthenics thing. However, Rough Strength is all about training without any luxuries or, in other words, with as little investment in equipment as possible. So ordering a weighted vest from the USA or Europe was a bad option for me. And by "bad" I mean expensive, of course.

Sometime later, I thought about making one myself. I drew some sketches, calculated how much weight I can add, thought about what to take as filler weight (sand or what?), etc. Yet all this remained as a project. So I decided to keep it simple and train calisthenics strength exercises with bodyweight only (ta-da!).

However, I came back to idea of weighted calisthenics because of lack of progress in some difficult exercises, but this time I discovered a much easier way. The backpack. First thought was: "Fuck, it was so obvious". But it is always like that in life. You think hard about things to come up with a really simple idea.

Here is a photo of my little beast and his friends:

The main problem was with what to put inside. Luckily, I have some generally useless objects that I can put in without any regret (on photo).

Of course, a backpack is not the same as a weighted vest. I probably cannot use it for Handstand work and sequences of exercises involving upside down positions of the body, but that is most likely it. Everything else can be successfully done weighted. So the obvious question is how to use this little dude to get stronger?

Weighted Calisthenics in Practice

There are generally two ways of using external weight in calisthenics movements:
- to make basic exercises harder
- to make easier transitions from one progression step to another

How to Make Basic Exercises Harder

I think all of you know that you can stay with your favorite bodyweight exercises longer, after you mastered them, if you add weight to them. The brilliance of this method is that you do not need to learn new movement patterns. If you mastered ring dips or ring chin-ups, then you can stay with them longer just by adding external weight. This will be good for building muscle. Why? It is because resistance is progressive, and the pattern is the same. One of the reasons why barbells are better for building muscle is the fact that the movement pattern stays the same.

Besides, you do not need to sacrifice exercises in which you feel your muscles the most, which is also great for hypertrophy. Often you can find that when you progress from exercise to exercise you may start feeling different muscles more. The only way to prevent this is to stay with the same exercise, but to make it harder. That is where weighted calisthenics can make big difference compared to pure bodyweight training. Here is me cranking out some reps in towel chin-ups (awesome exercise for grip strength) with added 8 kg [5].

However, if hypertrophy is not your concern, there is no need to bother. Or is there?

How to Make Easier Transitions from One Progression Step to Another

My primary goal is always strength. If you are trying to build strength with bodyweight exercises, you definitely have been in the situation where you have already mastered the progression step, but still cannot move to the next one. That is where weighted calisthenics are really handy. If you cannot progress from one step to the next, guess what, add weight and progress until you will be able to do this. This is relevant for static positions too. I often find that I progress well up to a 15 seconds hold. Further progress seems impossible. So why bother if I can just add weight, be in comfortable time range, and progress. I believe progress is all that matters. So adding weight might be the cure you are looking for. Here's a video of me doing a low ring assisted One-Arm Chin-Up with an additional 3.5 kg [6].

Closing Thoughts

Adding weight to bodyweight exercises is a powerful weapon. Use it wisely. Do not rush things. The fact that progressions can be easier does not mean that you can add more weight than you can handle. Slow and steady progress will always be better than meaninglessly adding large amounts of weight. Show some discipline and get results.

HOW TO ACHIEVE THE ONE-ARM HANDSTAND PUSH-UP

NOTICE: *To avoid any misunderstanding (and possible penis reduction in some individuals) by OAHSPU I mean a **wall-assisted** One-Arm Handstand Push-Up (or as many people prefer to call it One-Arm **Head**stand Push-Up). You kick up into handstand with feet resting on the wall. Take away one arm and lower down until your head touches the floor. Then push back up.*

So the theme of this article is the mighty One-Arm Handstand Push-Up – the move that many people consider impossible. And only few individuals around the world take all their determination into a fist and are training for it day in and day out. Are they out of their mind? Probably. Is it worth it? In my opinion, yes, and that is not because I am one of them. It is worth the time and effort because the OAHSPU is like the Holy Grail for me. It matches all of my requirements for an ultra-heavy, minimalistic, no-tech upper-body pushing exercise. It resonates with my inner self and its "impossibility" adds some more spice to it. This move undoubtedly requires your full concentration, lots of time, effort and hard work. This is what lures me to it. Are there better and safer ways to develop shoulder and triceps strength and size? Most definitely, but with all the safety you miss the romance of exploration.

Recently I was lucky enough to contact several people to provide some insights on the move. These people are Paul Wade, Jonathan Ferland-Valois and Logan Christopher. It is always educating to hear [read] different people's ideas especially if they are experts in the field (like these guys), so I figured out that it would be interesting to bring them all together and make some kind of a round table. I hope that you will learn something new from this multi-interview, and of course, I will not let you go without my own comments.

Let us get to the questions:

Introduce yourself. Tell us about your training experience.

Paul: My name is Paul John Wade. I began training nearly thirty-five years back, in my early twenties, when I was incarcerated in San Quentin. Virtually everything I learned about training, I learned from the crucible of prison. Prison has its own attitude, its own training culture, that is VERY different from the one most folks know beyond the bars. That was probably even truer back in the day.

Jonathan: Hi, my name is Jonathan Ferland-Valois. I'm 26 years old and I live in Canada. I have a fairly long training experience. I started gymnastics when I was 9 years old, and kept going until I was 21. After that I did my firefighting course during one year, which made me lose some of my previous abilities to some extent. I then participated in research about martial arts training (an unconventional type of training) and got into parkour. I kept doing that for a year, after which I decided to go on the road and live outside for a little while. I did that during 6 months, and landed in Vancouver with no money left, so I decided to stop and work a little bit. I had no preference concerning the type of job I was going to do and didn't want to have to beg to find work, so instead of sending copies of my resume everywhere, I took my gymnastics skills on the street to make some money right away, and out of luck, got hired by a small circus company by the same occasion. I then decided to stick with circus for a while, as it would be a good opportunity to learn more interesting things and take my time to develop my hand balancing skills furthermore.

Logan: My name is Logan Christopher and I've been called a physical culture renaissance man because I've practiced and gained decent ability in a wide range of different ways of working out. Some of my specialties include bodyweight training including some basic hand balancing and acrobatics, kettlebells and feats of strength.

Alex: To learn about me (what a shame if you have not already), you can read "About the Author" section of this book.

How did you learn about OAHSPU?

Paul: I first saw this move relatively late in my career, in my thirties. At the time, most of the pressing I was doing was built around one-arm pushups, elbow levers, and tricks based around the two. At the time, for me, an OAHSPU looked like a very different animal; I was kipping up into one-arm handstand from a one-arm elbow lever. I soon dropped that method and began learning and teaching the OAHSPU against the wall, the way you describe it, but with a kip from the legs.

The athlete I saw who performed this was an inmate, who spent a huge amount of time training alone in his cell. This was over many years, remember—no weights, not machines, no distractions. Just him and a wall. I teach this style over the elbow lever method, because it relies less on balance and skill. It's pure strength, baby.

Jonathan: I started thinking about it a while ago. Probably in 2006, year during which I often trained for up to 40 hours a week. I could crank up weighted HSPUs on the parallel bars, and wondered "what would I have to do to keep getting stronger if I no longer had access to a gymnastics gym with weights?" So that year, I kept doing weighted HSPUs and dips (with training partners hanging off my legs), and spent some time developing my one arm chin-up.

Logan: As it's discussed here, I first learned about it in Convict Conditioning. That being said, there are several similar skills involved in hand balancing that are equally amazing like pressing up from a one arm elbow lever to a one arm handstand.

Alex: I first learned about the OAHSPU, of course, from Convict Conditioning. This book changed my life and training approach forever. Before it, I thought that calisthenics are useless, and that you cannot build strength and muscle with their help. How wrong I was. When I dived into the world of progressive bodyweight training, I found out that it was what I was looking for. It fit my philosophy perfectly and even changed it a little bit. And for me OAHSPU is on the top of the pyramid of bodyweight exercises.

Is OAHSPU possible, in your opinion?

Paul: I have seen it performed with reasonable form by more than five individuals, and have performed it myself. Of course, it's possible. Sure, you won't see it on Youtube, but that's because very few folks train for it, and the ones who do almost never train for it over long periods. In this respect, it's kinda like the bent press. That used to be the number-one big lift a hundred years back, long before the bench press took over. In those days, Arthur Saxon could bent press over 400 pounds. But today—with better diets, steroids and so on—you won't see anyone on Youtube doing even half that. Does that mean it's impossible? No. It's just that very few people train for it today.

I have heard a gymnastics coach (who should've known better) say that he thought the OAHSPU was impossible, but remember that gymnasts don't train to perform this movement. So that's a little like a powerlifter saying that a double backflip is impossible. It's ignorance.

To work out whether it's humanly possible, don't listen to me. Just do the math. If you kip with the legs, a OAHSPU is not that far from an upside-down one-hand jerk—you are throwing up your bodyweight with one arm. That would be like a 200 pound guy pushing up 200 pounds with one arm. Is that possible? Hell, there are men who can do that much for ten reps. Obviously, the technique and balance is different, but the mechanical forces aren't all that dissimilar.

Modern athletes and wannabe athletes spend too much time on the internet, talking and thinking about training, and not enough time training. Your body is capable of far, far more than most folks give it credit for. As it stands now, the world record for the bench press is over 1076 pounds. People need to think about that for a little while, before declaring that a bodyweight OAHSPU is impossible.

Jonathan: If I didn't believe the OAHSPU to be possible, I wouldn't train on it the way I do now. But I want to make a little distinction. I doubt that it is possible to perform a good OAHSPU on the wall. To be balanced, a one-arm handstand need the center of mass to be inside the support zone (the hand). It means that your body have to tilt above your shoulder, which created an angle at the shoulder. Because of that, the wall would throw you off balance if you used it. Maybe it's possible to do it with the wall, but the form must look terrible.

Logan: Yes.

Alex: Of course, OAHSPU is possible. You can read my thoughts on this here – [7].

Do you train (for) OAHSPU right now? What's your progress?

Paul: Right now I'm way on the wrong side of fifty. When I was younger, I was pretty much obsessed with bodyweight presses. They were like a religion to me. But your attitudes change. As I get older, I am more and more into hand-balancing and equilibrium techniques. They are fun, and keep me strong, keeping my shoulders healthy. I couldn't perform a OAHSPU now, but that doesn't mean I couldn't if I specifically trained for it for a year or so.

I was recently inspired by getting in touch with Jack Arnow. Jack trained under Jasper Benincasa (of "CTI" fame). Those guys trained with bodyweight pulls the way I used to obsess over bodyweight presses. Jack is over seventy, but recently went to train with Al and Danny Kavadlo, and is still ridiculously strong. He's back in training for the one-arm pullup. He told me that Jasper Benincasa could still do a one-arm pullup in his eighties. Makes you think, huh? Maybe I should start training for it again.

Jonathan: As I said, I currently train to be able to do OAHSPUs, and I'm seeing consistent progress with it. I train it twice a week, and over the last year, I've been able to go from 3 reps with 3 fingers assistance to 5 reps with one finger assistance. Using the wall. I'm just waiting to be a bit stronger to practice it the same way, freestanding, basically the same way one would train for a one arm handstand: starting with a finger assistance, and then assisting less and less until the finger is no longer needed.

Logan: No, I do not. While I believe it is possible I know it is far beyond my capabilities at this time, which I think is true for most people. I would rather encourage people to work on full range handstand pushups then to go after the OASHPU. These will build strength in a full range of motion and are much more achievable. Another worthy goal is to work on freestanding handstand pushups.

Alex: Yes, I am training for OAHSPU right now. For the moment of publishing this book, I am doing triples in 5 finger assisted version. All in all it is a good progress for me considering that I am 85 kg and started with 5 finger assisted OAHSPU with partial range of motion (6 books).

What are prerequisites for starting OAHSPU training?

Paul: Great question. People who are not ready should not begin stressing the system by flipping upside down, and they should put the tissues of the shoulder under undue pressure. Before even thinking about these techniques, athletes should get used to inverse positions. Begin with exercises with the head down, like forward bends and stretches. Then move to headstands for a while. Then move to handstands against a wall. You need to let your blood vessels and vestibular system get used to being upside-down, so ease yourself into this training gradually.

You need strong shoulders to handle handstand pushups. I wouldn't even bother with them unless you are very comfortable with pullups and pushups already. Anyone's body can adapt to this training well, I promise. Just give it time.

Jonathan: The prerequisites for starting to train the OAHSPU are not perfectly clear yet, because as far as I know, nobody really achieved the skill (I choose to believe Paul Wade, but I don't think he did it with the form I want to see achieved) we're talking about. The prerequisites will become clearer as more people get it, if enough people ever make it for this skill to become a bit wider spread, which I doubt). So my advice would simply be to master the hardest exercises that you can possibly master before starting working the OAHSPU. You should definitely be able to do plenty of full range HSPUs. I don't think it's very useful to be able to do more than 20, but it's better than not doing enough. I think you should also make good use of gymnastics exercises like Planche, press to handstand, maltese, inverted cross. Doing good one arm push-ups would also help with triceps strength. Try to learn the regulation perfect one arm push-up; it will make a very good assistance exercise. One last thing: don't rush into it. I regularly search Google to find out if someone got it, and to see who's working on it, and I keep seeing fairly weak people claiming they're going to make it, or weak people trying to work on it while they can barely do wall headstand push-ups. I believe being able to do one arm handstands is very important, too. Do everything you can to get stronger first, then when you can't think of anything else that's easier than a one arm handstand push-up, you can start training it.

Logan: I would recommend someone work up to 15 full range handstand pushups in a single set before even beginning to work on this goal.

Alex: I will agree with all the participants to some degree. Of course, you need to master the regular HSPU first. As for going for 15-20 reps, I think it will work not for all the people. Let's take me for example. I have awesome progress in 1-8 rep range with 3-5 being ideal. It will be much more reasonable for me to find variations of HSPU that will give me more resistance than work on my endurance (8+ reps) to toothache. So when I hit, let's say, 3 sets of 8 reps in regular HSPU, I will be searching for the next progression step in order to get maximum results in minimum time.

Why so? Firstly, because different rep ranges suit different people. Secondly, different rep ranges use different energy storage. Finally, different rep ranges involve different muscle fibers more or less. Not to tire you with all the science, but what can you learn from this? In my case, progressing from 1 to 3 reps is hard. Progressing from 3-8 reps is much easier. But progressing from 8 to infinity a lot of times seems close to impossible. Besides, you can feel it. When I fail, for example, on the 5th rep, I feel that I lack strength. When I fail on 12th rep, I feel that I could go on and on, but my muscles are so pumped that I can't. You probably had similar experience.

So in conclusion, I'll say this: Try to work up to 15-20 regular HSPU, but if you struggle after 8-10 reps, then find a harder progression step like Diamond HSPU or Uneven HSPU (pictured on the previous page), or anything that works for you.

What are reasonable ways to achieve it? What progressions? How often?

Paul: Progression-wise, there are plenty of ways to skin a cat. Get real good with the two-arm handstand pushup first. Then move to a close grip. From here, there are lots of "transitional" techniques you can use to place more pressure on one-arm, like boxes, uneven hand positions, and so on. Once the one-arm is looking more possible you can bring in statics and partials. A great way to self-assist involves hooking the heels over a low wall, and curling yourself up with the hamstrings on one-arm. That's a powerful assistance technique, but you need to know what you are doing. Personally, I don't favor negatives, especially when you are coming down on your noggin.

As regards frequency, I am a little contrary to the usual advice here. I prefer hard workouts—say 10 maximum attempts, if you are advanced—then lots of rest. Two times per week is fine. For some people, even less frequency will be better. You grow when you rest kid, not when you train.

Jonathan: Definitely not negatives. I tried it, and it didn't work. I think the most reasonable way to achieve it is to first get proficient at regular HSPUs (full range) on various supports (edge of a high object, parallel bars, rings), and also get pretty good one arm push-ups. Learn to do Planches, too. The stronger your shoulders, upper back and triceps [are], the more chances you have to succeed. Then you have to start working with a decreasing assistance. I use my fingers, and I find it works pretty well. I don't have it yet, but I'll see. If it's not good enough, I'll just change my training techniques do adapt. The way I do it is that I pick a level of assistance with which I can only do 1-2 reps, then I build up the reps until I can do 10-12. Once I can do that, I decrease the assistance again. As to how often, it depends on everybody's training. Adjust the frequency to the volume you're doing and to your ability to recover. I train it twice a week, doing up to 10 sets with a lot of rest if it's low reps. After that, I do Planche push-ups (I recently added Planche press to handstand as well) and one arm push-ups. Someone who would like to train it every day should probably stick with 1-3 sets per training. But it depends the intensity. When I do my sets, I avoid going to failure, but I'm pretty damn close, and once in a while, I do fail to complete a rep.

Here is video of Jonathan performing 2 Finger-Assisted OAHSPU – [8]

Logan: Considering no one has done it yet this is all just theory. The approach I would take is to go up on the finger tips of the off hand and gradually take them away. Since a lot of pressure can still be used through one finger I would also position the finger further away from the body. This will help the strength but balance as well. I would attempt to do this as often as possible without doing too much work.

Alex: There are really lots of ways to achieve OAHSPU. Finger assisted is only one of them. You can do partials. You can take something sliding, put your assisting hand on it and assist while pressing up with other. Or you can try something like on the photo below:

Opportunities are endless. Frequency-wise, I used something similar to Jonathan, but it is clearly too much for me. Once per week works awesome though.

What are your personal tips for the OAHSPU?

Paul: Make it as easy as you can. You can use a wall to limit balance requirements, but a corner is better for stability. Learn the art of kipping (kicking up) with the legs to make the take off easier. Apart from this, learn to be explosive in the push off, the hardest part, with lots of clapping handstand work against the wall. Learning back and front flips will help with shoulder explosiveness, and I will show people how to learn these techniques progressively in *Convict Conditioning 3*. These tips will make the movement significantly more attainable.

Jonathan: Take your time to do it well. Learn every little thing you got to learn. Remember, officially, nobody's achieved the movement. It means that it's hard as fuck. Another advice is to take care of your body. Don't get hurt. Listen to yourself. Avoid inflammation in your shoulders, elbows or wrists. It is true that there's a race for the first person to get it. [It's] not an official race, but I'm sure that every guy trying to get it wants to be the first. I know I do. But no matter what, the most important is to just finish it. It's useless to wreck your body just to be the first. Even if someone [else] gets it first, I'll still be happy. I hope I'll do it first... But I'll be happy, because I'll know for sure it's possible, and it's going to help many people take a big step forward, I'm sure.

Logan: Unless you're in the circus I wouldn't even go for it.

Alex: Here are some of my thoughts:

- If you already mastered regular HSPU but any assisted OAHSPU version is too hard for you, try limiting range of motion. Use books to monitor your progress. Who reads them nowadays anyway, right? (This is a joke) I was using this method myself. At first, I could not do 5-finger assisted OAHSPU. So I put 6 books under my head. Any time I hit 3 sets of 5 I took away one book and worked up to this volume again.

- As for finger-assisted version, be careful with your fingers. Do not rush things. If you finished all the reps with five fingers for the first time, perform couple of more sessions and only then try 4-finger assisted version.

- In any progression, do not forget to shift your weight on the working arm. It should feel like Dumbbell or Kettlebell Side Press because of the weight shift.

- Try to spread your legs in Handstand position. This will lower your center of mass and will make the exercise a little bit easier.

- Obviously, take your time. To learn this feat, you will need A LOT of time.

What are your thoughts on carryover between OAHSPU and freestanding HS and HSPU?

Paul: There obviously is some. But we are really talking apples and oranges, Alex. Freestanding is largely skill-based and depends on the ability of your nervous system and vestibular system. The OAHSPU is more about raw muscle and tendon strength.

I have seen men who were very, very powerful in handstand pressing against a wall, who could not hold a free handstand. Likewise, I have seen some talented hand-balancers who could walk all day on their hands who were not that strong in real terms.

Jonathan: Freestanding handstands should be easy by the time you work on your OAHSPUs. I think you have no business training it if you can't do a solid handstand. For the carryover from OAHSPU to HSPUs, well, the HSPUs should feel much easier than they did before. Being able to do OAHSPUs won't make you much [have more endurance] for doing

HSPUs if you can already do 20 or more, I think. But if you can do several OAHSPUs, well… you'll also be able to do more HSPUs. I guess we'll have to see when someone gets it. The same [goes] for the carryover to overhead pressing. We'll know when people start doing tests. I think that a good test would be to achieve a full range OAHSPU (on handbalancing canes, per example) first, for a solid 5 reps. At that point, you'd have tree trunks instead of arms. And then, test your 1 RM with military press. Train it for 2 weeks. Test your 1 RM again, and see how much it improved after you've gotten more used to the movement.

Logan: I imagine the strength and balance will help to some degree. Nothing would work as well as just spending time on those specific exercises though.

Alex: Well, I've seen a little carryover from training full ROM HSPU to the Handstand, but nothing from OAHSPU training. Maybe I need to work up to more reps. And I haven't seen any effect other way around.

Your final advice to those brave ones that desire to learn OAHSPU? You can add any thoughts that were not covered earlier.

Paul: The best advice really isn't training advice. It's about perspective. Approaching a OAHSPU is kinda like approaching a 500 pound bench press. It's an elite strength feat. If you want to do it, raw and drug-free, you can. But it is gonna take years and years of solid, focused work. The only reason folks think a 500 bench is possible is that everyone in the gym benches. Relatively few athletes these days, the world over, train for the OAHSPU. That's the only difference.

It makes me laugh, Alex. Nobody would get under a 500 pound bar and try to bench press it for a couple months, fail, and then assume it was impossible, right? That'd be dumb. But I get messages from athletes all the time saying they have "tried" the OAHSPU and think it's impossible. I tell them; "it's not impossible—you're not strong enough! Train for it specifically for ten years, then come back and tell me it's impossible."

Jonathan: If you're ready for it, go for it. Stick with it for a long time. If you don't, you won't improve very much. Stay focused, and good luck!

Logan: It may be helpful to also work with exercises besides the OAHSPU to help you towards your goal. Incline one arm pushups would probably help. I would also advise lifting a heavy dumbbell overhead. If you could set one up to hang at head height so you're working a partial like in the OAHSPU you could easily add weight overtime. Since the body position will be different it may not have too much carryover but it could help. This would be something worth testing out.

Alex: Do not rush it and stay focused.

Where can Rough Strength readers find more information about you and your training approach?

Paul: The first *Convict Conditioning* book is a great place to start, but I would also wholeheartedly recommend anything by Al Kavadlo if folks want to break into progressive calisthenics. He also has a huge volume of instructional posts and videos he has put out for free to help bodyweight students. We are looking to spread information through the *Progressive Calisthenics Certification (PCC)*, which is an amazing project we have been working on for a couple years now.

Luckily, as time passes there are more and more sites with good information about bodyweight strength. I want to thank you for spreading the word about old school calisthenics, Alex. Rough Strength is an awesome site, and I hope folks out there take the opportunity to train with you and learn from you.

Jonathan: Rough Strength readers can find more information about me and my training approach on wandererstraining.com. I don't have many articles out yet, but over time, there will be more.

Logan: My main website is http://LegendaryStrength.com where they can find much more on hand balancing, bodyweight training, and a whole bunch more.

Closing Thoughts

Thanks to Paul, Jon and Logan for their input. It was awesome. As for you, my precious reader, I hope you have learnt a thing or two. Maybe you even got inspired to try to tame the mighty OAHSPU. If so, I encourage you to try it. Be brave. Do what you want, not what others say you should.

10 TIPS FOR MASTERING THE PERFECT ONE-ARM PUSH-UP

The Perfect One-Arm Push-Up – many claim to be able to perform it, still there is almost no video proof to back up those claims. Why so? Firstly, everybody has ego. Claiming that you can do such a complex skill like the Perfect One-Arm Push-Up [POAPU] boosts that ego like nothing else. There is no harm in bragging, unless you cannot back up your words.

Secondly, it is surprisingly easy to get trapped in improper technique with this skill. You can see lots of videos of the One-Arm Push-Up, but 99% of them are half-assed-twisted-body-feet-wide-pseudo-push-ups. That is not what we are discussing here. That exercise has almost nothing in common with real One-Arm Push-Up, and it is a walk in the park compared to our beast. Many people push this shitty technique as POAPU, but do not be fooled. They just do not have the patience to gain the strength required for this move. Thus, they can forget about achieving anything great. Lots of people also do not believe POAPU can be done the proper way, but that is not true. It definitely can be achieved, but the process will require lots of time, hard work, and patience.

Now let us take a closer look to see what the hell the Perfect One-Arm Push-Up is.

What Is a Perfect One-Arm Push-Up?

This question is highly debatable. Everybody has his own criteria for "perfection" of the One-Arm Push-Up. Anyway, I will give you *my* personal requirements for proper technique. Here is a list:
- The shoulders should be parallel to the ground
- The feet should be not wider than shoulder-width
- The twist of the body should be minimal
- The body should be straight (looking from the side)
- You should lower yourself down until there is no more than 10 cm between the ground and your chest

If you do not meet even just one requirement, then you should reconsider your technique, stop fooling around, and start training the real One-Arm Push-Up.

How Have I Learnt about It?

I have learnt about the possibility of the One-Arm Push-Up a long time ago. I was just starting training at that time. I remember exactly the moment when after a set of push-ups my dad came up and asked me: "Can you do it with one arm?" And I was like: "Why not?" Of course, I failed miserably. However, after couple of attempts I figured out that if I spread my legs really wide, twist to the side, and lower only half the way, I can do it. With a feeling of accomplishment, but in reality accomplishing nothing, I happily forgot about the skill for some time.

Many years later I was lucky enough to read one book that changed it all. That was Convict Conditioning. In one of its sections, Paul Wade (author) wrote about the Perfect One-Arm Push-Up. I considered myself pretty strong at that time. "Bench pressing 120 kg for sets of 4, man, I should be able to crush that bodyweight thing" – I believed. Again, I got another reality check and deep understanding and appreciation for heavy calisthenics. From that moment, my fight with POAPU began.

NOTE: Many people call this skill Prisoner Push-Up (popularized after Convict Conditioning). I am OK with it, but will use my term anyway.

What Muscles Does It Work?

Honestly, I do not questions like these. "Hey, dude, will it work my biceps?" or "What can I do to work my rear delts?" You know what I mean. However, I shall make an exception for this exercise. Why? Because it is quite interesting in this aspect, as well as any high level calisthenics exercise.

The Perfect One-Arm Push-Up is a horizontal push. So we can expect that it works our pecs, front delts and triceps. From experience, I can say that triceps stimulation is the most significant. Second place is shared by the front delts and, wait for it, your lats. How unexpected is that? This happens due to the high demand for body stabilization. Then come your pecs. In the Bench Press, which is also horizontal push, the lats work as stabilizers, but you cannot feel them as much, and so you primarily feel either the pecs, front delts, or triceps.

NOTE: Of course, everything written in previous paragraph is just my experience. You can feel it differently. Who cares, anyway?

Why Train for It?

Because it is awesome. Not enough? How about insane core and body stability and inhuman pushing strength? Maybe increased arm size as well as hypertrophy in the entire upper body will interest you? What about a stronger grip? Add to the mix the fact that all you need for training is the floor. You can find it everywhere unless you are falling from the sky. So the advantages are obvious for me.

The Main Question

Now just ask yourself this question: "Is it worth the effort?" If you doubt even for a split-second, then forget about it, go play the "Daughters-Mothers" (a popular girls' game here in Ukraine) and call it a day. If your answer is "Hell-fucking-yes!", then read on.

10 Tips to Master the Perfect One-Arm Push-Up

1. What are the prerequisites? Or rather, when should you consider starting to learn the POAPU? Well, it is not that easy to answer this question, but let us be reasonable. You should be able to do somewhere around 20+ Diamond Push-Ups, 10+ wall-assisted Handstand Push-Ups, and 3-5 Full ROM wall-assisted Handstand Push-Ups. Then you can start, but you need to progress...

2. ...slow and steady. I cannot emphasize this enough. You can learn the POAPU only very slowly due to the highly demanding nature of this skill. Let me give you an example. I was talking with one highly known Ukrainian powerlifter one day and mentioned the POAPU in conversation. He said: "Hey, I can try it". Here are couple of details:

- He had a body weight of 93 kg at that time
- He bench pressed raw 170 kg for double couple of days ago and I was spotting him (so he's pretty strong)

I explained him all the technique points and he got into POAPU starting position. He tried to do the repetition and after heavy struggle, he finally has got one very shaky ugly rep. Why am I telling this? Yes, he had no skill in this move, he tried it for the first time and in couple of weeks/months he could do an easy 5. However, the main point is that even a high-level powerlifter (that can bench press 2 times his bodyweight, raw and for reps) struggled big time with this move. So if you are not in that category, I advise you to start as slow and light as possible.

3. Always shift your weight to the working arm. Sounds simple, but, then again it is very easy to get carried away and end up with shitty technique and no strength. Lots of progression exercises will involve two arm work. One arm will be as close to the POAPU position as possible, and will be doing all the work. The second one will be assisting. This type of progression will work only on one condition: your working arm should do the majority of work and the assisting arm should only *assist*. Otherwise, you will fail.

4. Vary the progressions. I have noticed that with the POAPU the issue of training variety is critically important. Oftentimes increasing strength with one type of progression becomes really hard very soon. So it is wise to vary them or to use several in one training cycle. What progressions to use?

5. Here are some example progressions. There are two main issues in learning the POAPU: front delt/triceps/lat/pec strength and core strength. The latter can be trained by simply holding the proper top position of the Perfect One-Arm Push-Up and it is rarely an issue. It is the easier of the two. The delt/triceps/lat/pec strength requires a progressive approach where we use the resistance from the easiest to hardest until we can do a push-up solely with one arm.

I can divide the learning approaches into three:
- The one with changing the body's position in space
- The one with the assisting arm
- Others

The one with changing the body position in space. This is simple. If you cannot perform the POAPU on the floor, use the surface that is higher. For example, a couch, table, or even a wall. Find the one that is suitable for your current levels of strength and start from there.

The one with an assisting arm. You will be in actual POAPU position and will assist with your non-working arm. Again, there are several ways to do it. I can think of four reasonable ones.

The first way is *finger assisted*. You get into the POAPU position and place the fingertips of your assisting hand close to you. When you get stronger just use less and less fingers, like 5, 4, 3 etc.

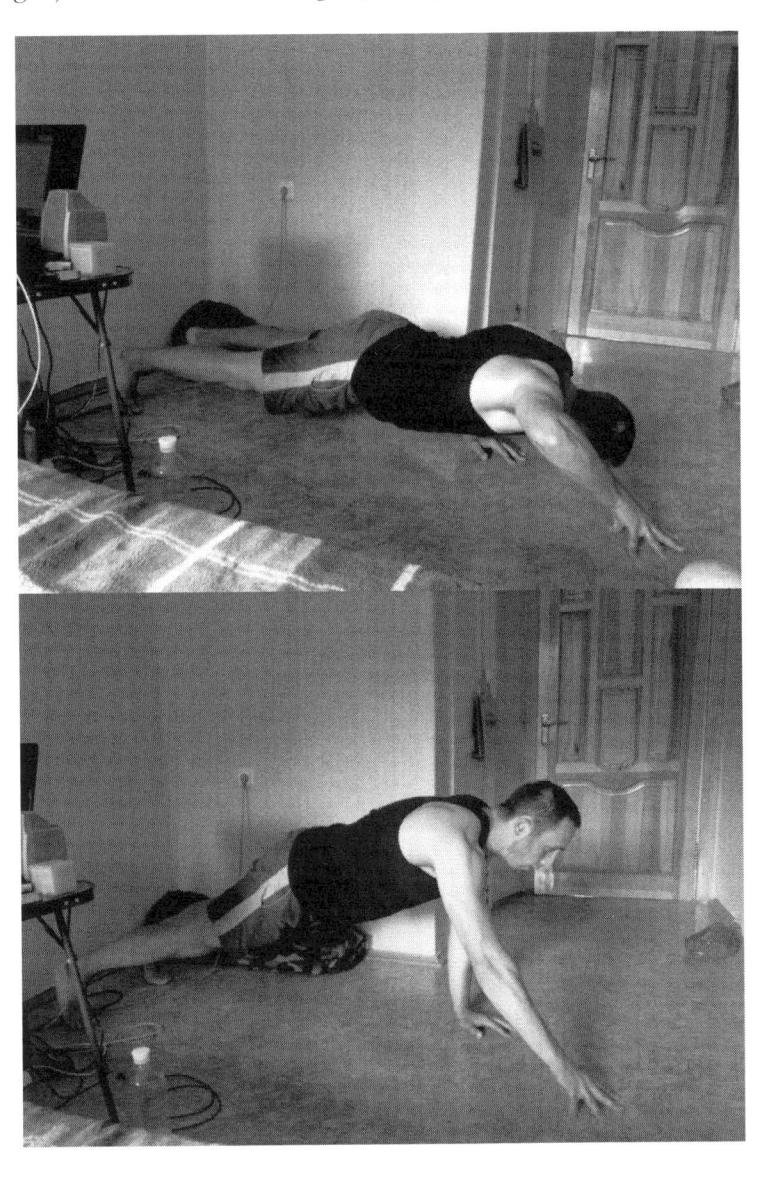

The second way is *towel assisted*. Get into the POAPU position on a slick surface. Put a towel near you and place your assisting hand on it. As you lower down you just slide the towel forward and when you push up - slide it back. The main point here is to hold your assisting arm locked in the elbow throughout the whole movement.

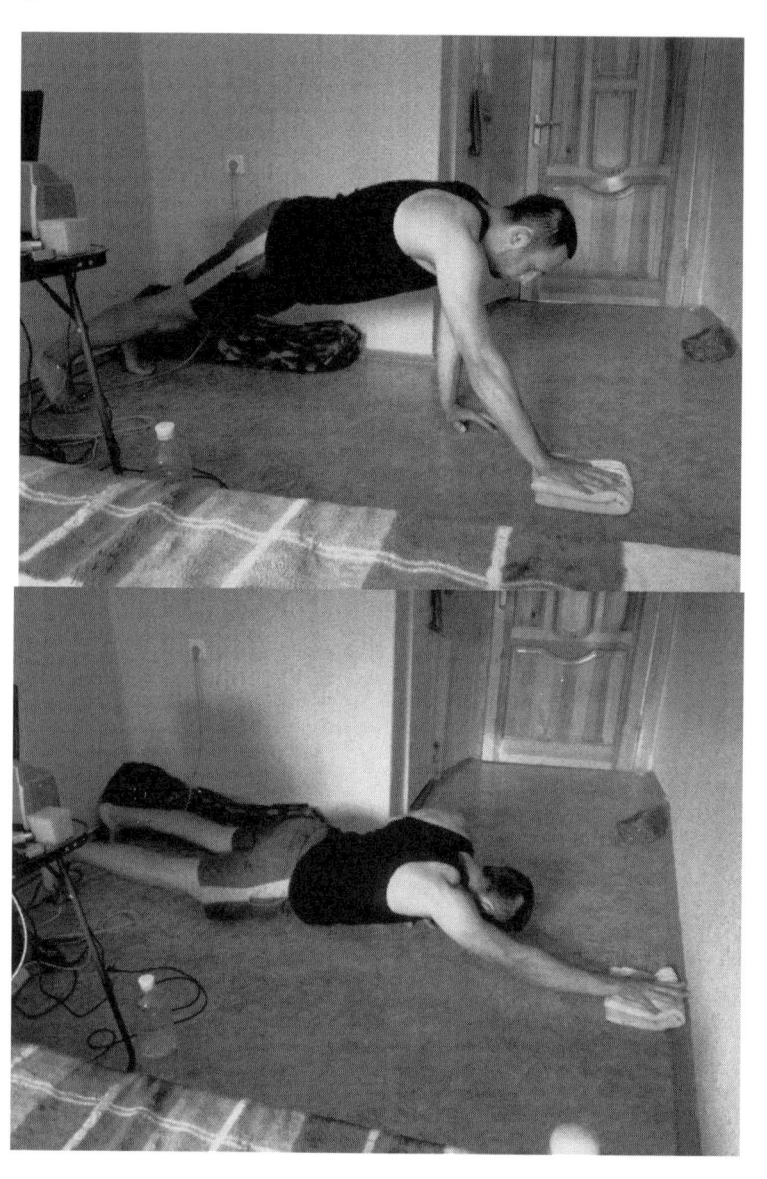

The third way is a *mix of both the finger and towel assisted versions*. The same as the second, but instead of your whole hand, you put only fingertips on the towel.

The fourth way is to hold onto a *gymnastic ring* with your assisting arm at shoulder height. As you lower down just slide the ring to the side. It is similar to the towel assisted version, but feels a bit different. Again, the elbow of your assisting arm should be locked throughout the whole move.

The others (my classification is awesome as always). In this category, you can put any other reasonable progression. For example, a *band assisted version*. Put the resistance band under your chest. As you lower down, it will support you and decrease the resistance.

Another choice would be *leg progression*. If you can do POAPU with your feet wide, you can progress through decreasing the feet width.

And, of course, do not forget the *partials*. Put some books under your chest to decrease the range of motion. Once you get stronger, just take out one book and start over.

I think I gave enough progressions to keep you busy for some time.

6. You need to follow a set/rep prescription for strength. 3 sets of 5, 5 sets of 3, 4 times 4, 4 sets of 2, 6 sets of 1 etc. There are lots of reasonable schemes. In addition, you can use a more flexible scheme of total reps (described earlier in the book). For example, perform a total of 15 reps in 5 repetition maximum exercise. So your session can look something like this:

Set 1: 4 reps (I prefer to leave one in the tank)
Set 2: 4 reps
Set 3: 3 reps (things get harder)
Set 4: 2 reps
Set 5: 2 reps.
Total: 15 reps.

7. How often? This is another tricky question. Everybody is different, so you will need to experiment to determine the frequency that works for you. Start training it once per week. Do it for 4-6 weeks. Then try twice per week. Stick to this frequency for 4-6 weeks. Then compare the results. Pick the one that turned out to be the best. You may also experiment with 3 times per week, but in this case, you will need to balance intensity and cut the volume.

8. How to include the POAPU work into a program? Do you remember the "What Muscles..." section? The POAPU is a horizontal push. Here is a couple of thoughts on programming:

- If you want to get good at it, you need to put it first.
- You can alternate POAPU work with One-Arm Chin-Up work.
- Basically, you can switch any horizontal push exercise for POAPU

work.

- If you train POAPU once per week, it is reasonable to stick to one progression for 4-6 weeks.

- If you train POAPU twice or 3 times per week, it is good to use different progressions on different days.

9. *When to progress?* A good rule of right time for making it to the next step I learnt from Mike Mahler. When you can do 2 reps more than you need on the last set, it is time to go further. If you need to do 3 sets of 5 and you can do 7 reps in the last set, add resistance for the next session.

10. *What is next?* So we will assume that you have mastered the Perfect One-Arm Push-Up. How can you progress further? Several ways come to my mind:

- *Add weight.* Straight and simple. You can use a weighted vest, chains, bands or a backpack.

- *Elevate your feet.* This will definitely make the POAPU harder. Work your way up until you end with OAHSPU.

- *Try the fingertip version.* You will gain incredible strength in your fingers. If you are brave enough, you can work up to Claw Fingertip Perfect One-Arm Push-Ups (more on this later in this section).

- *Mix of the above.* Screw it all and try the Weighted Feet-Elevated Claw Fingertip Perfect One-Arm Push-Up (notice how good I am in creating pointless long names for exercises)

Is It Reasonable to Use Weights to Learn the POAPU?

Nothing will be better in learning the POAPU than actual practice of the skill. With this in mind you can try to add assistance exercises with weights. However, it all depends on the individual. Some will benefit, while others will see no difference.

Try adding One-Arm Kettlebell Floor Presses, or use a dumbbell if you like. In addition, Military Presses will not be a waste of time.

Closing Thoughts

What can I say in conclusion? The Perfect One-Arm Push-Up is the skill that requires lots of patience and hard work. Not everybody will be dedicated and disciplined enough to earn this skill. However, those who will still manage to push through all the obstacles will acquire the skill that very tiny amount of the Earth population has. Then comes the bragging part. Nevertheless, remember, you cannot brag unless you grow a beard or at least mustache. That is it.

PRACTICAL TIPS TO IMPROVE YOUR PULL-UP PERFORMANCE

So one day you woke up and thought: "Hey! How many fake world endings did I live through? Maybe I need to improve my Pull-Up performance to be at least somewhat cooler the next time?" Well, this might not be the actual thought, but why not? The Pull-Up is an essential exercise for building strength and muscle. It is hard to find an exercise that can match the regular Pull-Up in terms of building pulling strength. Besides, it requires nothing except your bodyweight. It is not a coincidence that this exercise is a staple in the training of military and law enforcement units.

Now let us take a closer look at this move. You can see basic performance of the Pull-Up in the pictures.

There are several rules for performing the move:
- Start from a dead hang
- Touch the bar with your chest at the top

Of course, there are several other rules like keeping your shoulders back and in their sockets, as well as keeping your lower back arched, but these requirements can vary from individual to individual. In addition, there are several hand placement considerations:
- Palms facing the bar are generally called "pull-ups". These are

considered "tough" pull-ups here in Ukraine. However, in reality they just shift the accent from your biceps to your forearm muscles a little bit.

- Palms facing you are regarded as "Chin-Ups".
- Palms facing each other are called "Neutral Grip Pull-Ups".

These terms could be used interchangeably. There are also Ring Chin-Ups. They mix all of the hand placements, because rings allow free wrist rotation. They are the most wrist friendly of them all.

As for hand placement width, common dogma says that the wider the grip, the more the lats are working, and the closer the grip the more biceps work. Well, Close Grip Pull-Ups definitely work your biceps more. However, I cannot agree with the wide grip statement. According to the latest research [9], lat activation is pretty similar in middle-grip and wide grip Pull-Ups. The wide-grip version definitely lacks range of motion though. My advice is do not waste your time on the wide grip version and concentrate on regular Chin-Ups instead.

Ok, everybody should already know this. Let us get to the fun part.

The Fun Part

So how do you improve these bad boys? There are several practical ways that depend on your conditions.

First of all, if you are just working toward your first Pull-Up, then you should concentrate on different assisted variations. They could be band-assisted Pull-Ups, feet elevated Pull-Ups, Pull-Ups with a partner's help, and Pull-Up negatives. You should get your first rep pretty fast if you are not very overweight or a struggling-even-to-pick-up-the-pen weakling. You can get there by trying Pull-Ups every day, or by hitting them hard once or twice per week. Anyway, when you get to sets of 3-5 reps everything will become a bit different. You may find that you are not progressing at all. That is when you should apply "greasing the groove". It means that you should perform Pull-Ups throughout the day without draining yourself. Therefore, if your maximum is 5 reps, try doing one set of 2-3 reps several times per day. You should get to 10-12 reps in no time.

There are several ways to go from here. You can either add weight and get stronger progressing further towards One-Arm Chin-Ups, or you can work on endurance, or both. Specialization will get you more results though. If you decide to get stronger, then I recommend not exceeding five reps in a set. You should be working in low to moderate volume. Schemes like 3 x 3, 3 x 5, 4 x 4, 5 x 3, 5 x 5, etc., would be just right. Try to add weight whenever possible. If you pick endurance training, then there is good old high frequency training to help you. Try to perform one set to failure in the morning and one set to failure in the evening. After 3 weeks, give yourself several days of rest and then repeat.

In addition, it would not be a bad idea to train your grip. Try to add some hangs from the bar here and there. This should help.

Closing Thoughts

Now you have all the info you need to improve your Pull-Up numbers. Do not waste your time. Start training right now!

10 TIPS FOR LEARNING THE HANDSTAND

I always get a lot of questions on handstand training. The most popular of them is: "How to obtain the free-standing handstand?" Well, this question is too broad to answer it with a couple of words (actually, I could answer with one - "practice", but this will leave you with almost nothing). So I decided to share my experience and useful tips on how to obtain this spectacular feat of strength and balance.

The Handstand

The Handstand is easily one of the most impressive strength feats out there. Actually, there is only one feat that is cooler than the Handstand - the One-Arm Handstand. With all seriousness, the Handstand requires decent strength in shoulders and arms, and particularly in forearms and fingers. In addition, it will require great tension in your whole body, as well as precise body awareness in the upside-down position.

Also, the Handstand can be different. There are several variations of it, for example, the straddle, tuck, pike and regular version. However, I want to emphasize form here. The Handstand can be straight and arched. Straight is harder. It requires decent shoulder flexibility, hand and core strength, but it is worth the effort because it is easier to learn One-Arm Handstand from straight version rather than from arched.

Sig Klein's arched handstand

Yuval Ayalon's straight handstand [10]

According to Ido Portal, it is almost impossible to learn the "one-armer" from arched or "banana" Handstand. Therefore, it is better to learn straight version at initial stage. You might not be able to crush it right away due to it being so demanding (especially if your bodyweight is 80+ kg and you lack shoulder and hip flexibility). Do not get frustrated though. Learn the arched version first, and then learn the straight one. Learning the straight version is about understanding Hollow Body Position. It would be a great idea to spend some time learning and researching this position to perform it perfectly while standing on your hands. In addition, you need to work on your shoulder mobility and flexibility big time. This is much harder than it sounds. Lack of flexibility may be the single most important problem you need to address in the quest for a straight Handstand.

Here is a good self-correcting exercise to straighten your Handstand [11]. Get into Face to Wall Handstand. Place your hands as close to the wall as possible, but without falling out. Touch the wall only with your toes and preferably upper chest.

How Did I Learn the Handstand?

Well, I learnt it the hard way. At some point, I thought that I would never be able to hold it without the wall. However, I can do it now and so will be able you. Here are 10 tips for you to obtain this awesome skill:

1. Push through your fingers. I cannot emphasize on this more. *The key to holding a handstand is pushing through your fingers.* Here are two photos (I have used soft material to illustrate what finger pressure is):

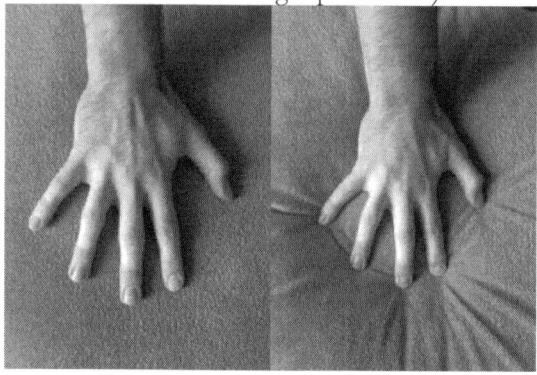

The first one - no finger pressure, second - finger pressure. You should always apply this technique while holding a Handstand. Again, this is the key to finding a balance.

2. Work on Handstand Push-Ups. I have seen really good carry over in the training of free-standing Handstands from full range of motion Handstand Push-Ups. You will build the necessary strength in shoulders and triceps with this dynamic movement. So you can focus on balance more.

3. You need to find that "sweet spot". You will quickly notice that you can easily hold a freestanding Handstand for a couple of seconds when you find that position where the center of mass is approximately above your knuckles.

4. Use spotter when possible. The quick way to learn freestanding Handstand is to practice it with a spotter. He or she should give the right amount of assistance for you not to fall out of equilibrium - not more, not less. This is probably the most beneficial way to practice Handstand as you learn correct position from the start.

5. Practice Kick-Ups. It can be easy for you to hold a Handstand, but you might not be able to kick-up in it every time. No big deal. Work on Kick-Ups. Kick up, hold it for a second or two, get down, then repeat.

6. Use high frequency. Handstand training requires a lot of repetition. So it would be a good idea to practice it daily. However, not to failure. If you feel that you just cannot hold it today no matter what you do, then, of course, it is time for some rest. With practice, you will find out when it is time to train Handstand and when it is better to rest. Of course, with increasing intensity or volume you will need to cut frequency a bit.

7. Do not skip steps in progression. It will be tempting to hold a freestanding Handstand right away. Some "coaches" will tell you to do that, but that is wrong. Principles of progressive resistance work here as well. You need to hold Wall-Assisted Handstand for at least several sets of 30 sec before moving to next intermediate step - Wall-Spotted Handstand. Then work to sets of at least 20 sec of that. Then you may play with the freestanding version. That is just the basic progression. Some individuals will need more steps, some - less.

8. Work on both Wall-Assisted Handstand versions. You need to work on Back-to-Wall and Face-to-Wall Handstands equally. They both have their advantages and disadvantages and complement each other perfectly.

9. Overcome the fear of falling. There will be fear of falling first couple of times. Do not worry; you WILL fall. You will fall many times if you are into this hand-balancing thing. It is part of the process. Learn some ways to get out of Handstand if something goes wrong. This will add some confidence. However, the best and fastest way to overcome the fear of falling is just to do that damn Handstand again and again. Until you have the confidence. Again, a spotter will be useful in this situation.

10. Practice more. There is nothing better for learning a skill than practice. So practice, practice, practice and then practice some more.

Here is yours truly doing some hand balancing – [12]. My Handstand is far from perfect, but there is always room for improvement.

Closing Thoughts

The process of learning the Handstand was not easy. It took me a lot more time than it would have taken if I knew what I know now. So do not repeat my mistakes. Read, absorb and use this information to get that Handstand finally. Put in hard work and reap the benefits.

ONE-ARM CHIN-UP TIPS

The One-Arm Chin-Up.

I cannot be more official because it is the skill that everyone admires (or at least should admire). The true master of the One-Arm Chin-Up possesses such biceps and lats, for their bodyweight of course, that all conventional bodybuilders silently stand in the corner, cry, and burn from envy. He obtains arm strength to match that size.

Some people think that this feat of strength is out of reach, especially heavyweight ones. This is not true. I heard of at least two persons that are approx. 100 kg (220 lb).

Anyway, let us get back to the tips.

Train Mostly with Singles

If you can make sustainable progress, it is better to train with singles. Here is the logic behind this statement. The One-Arm Chin-Up is a complex feat of strength. It has lots of details to work on. Different parts of the move require individual attention. It is not some low-skill exercise like the Lat Pulldown or the Bench Press. It is a completely different kind of beast.

It is obvious that your initial goal should be completing just one perfect repetition, hence the feat of strength category. That is why it is beneficial to train yourself in a feat-of-strength way with singles. However, it will work only if you can divide the whole progression into really small steps.

One of the best ways to implement singles is Rest-Pause Training. Let me explain it to you. Pick a progression step that is fairly hard, but you can do three perfect reps in. Perform single rep with right arm. Rest for 30 seconds. Then perform a single rep with the left arm. Rest for 30 seconds, and so on until you hit 5-6 singles per arm. After that, call it a day. Return 5-7 days later and repeat (the amount of required rest will vary from individual to individual). Usually it would take a couple training sessions to hit 10 singles per arm. You have several options after that. You can either shave off 5 seconds from the rest periods and work back up to 10 singles per arm, or you can pick a bit harder variation and start over with 5-6 singles.

In addition, you should understand several things:

1. A single repetition consists of 4 phases: bottom hold, positive phase, top hold, negative phase. The time required for completion of all these phases combines into a total called "time under tension". When we are working with singles, it is important to understand that progress can be measured in different ways, and increased time under tension is one of them. So if you struggle with adding sets or intensity, do not forget that you always can increase time under tension.

2. Rest-Pause in not the only way to progress in singles.

3. Singles are always hard. For One-Arm Chin-Up training, it is ultra-true. Adding reps may seem impossible sometimes, but you can always use the classic singles-to-reps progression scheme. It looks like this: at first, you work on increasing number of single-rep sets. Once you hit 8-10 sets of 1, you can try a couple of sets of 2. Work up to 6-8 sets of 2 reps, and then try couple of sets of 3. After this point, your progress should be a bit easier (or not). When to use it? Obviously, after you got your first full rep and during getting it when you need to build up assisted or partial reps to progress further

Pick the Progression That Is the Most Effective for You

There are tons of progressions toward the One-Arm Chin-Up. The most effective are considered rope or towel assisted, finger assisted, and rock climbers'. Rope assisted is the best for me. I can always carry the rope in my bag. It feels the most natural. The main thing is that with rope assistance you can adjust intensity similarly to the barbell. Just count the fists on the rope and you are all set. It is very comfortable for me.

Pick a progression that suits you, but do not forget that the best progress often can be achieved through mixing different approaches.

Don't Hit It Too Often

The One-Arm Chin-Up is not that exercise that you want to overdo.

Firstly, you cannot progress fast in it. Secondly, frequent training carries an increased risk of injury. Once a week works awesome for me. You should experiment to find out what is best for you.

Additionally, depending on the intensity you can handle, you can add more frequent work and see how it affects your progress. For example, if you can do partial OACU reps (2/3 of range of movement and harder) and weighted negatives, you can try adding bodyweight negatives every day and see what impact it will make to your progress.

One-Arm Negatives and Static Hangs

One-Arm Chin-Up Negatives are quite a powerful tool in your arsenal if used properly. How to use them?

1. Count the time of the come down. 6-12 seconds are optimal for me.

2. Add weight to them when you hit at least 3 sets of 12 seconds per arm.

3. If you do not want to add weight, you can pause at different points of the descent. My preference is the One-Arm Chin-Up Negative with a 5-second hold at the top, a 5-second hold at 90 degrees, and 5-second hold in the flexed hang (near the bottom of the movement).

4. In addition, you can mix the assisted positive phase with full the negative. For example, you can perform Rope Assisted OACU, but at the top, release assisting hand and perform full OACU Negative. This is a good intermediate step in learning the OACU.

5. Finally, do not forget to devote similar attention to all the parts of the descent. Do not hold the top position too much because it is the easiest, and do not drop at the bottom without reaching a full hang.

In my opinion, One-Arm Static Holds are also very useful. The bottom hang is useful for grip strength and endurance. The 90-degree hang is useful for strength in the middle part of OACU and moving past the sticking point. The top hang is generally useful in One-Arm Chin-Up work. Practice them, but do not overdo it.

That is all. I hope it will help you in your quest for the One-Arm Chin-Up.

CLAW FINGERTIP PUSH-UPS

So you woke up one day and thought: "Man, it's going to be awesome to have strong fingers!" Well, maybe that is not the exact story. Maybe, you were upset because your girlfriend defeated you in arm wrestling. Or you saw that video where the guy punches a watermelon with his two fingers and leaves two holes in it. If you do not believe me, just search "watermelon challenge" on YouTube.

It does not really matter how you came to this. What matters is the fact that grip and finger strength are very important. No matter what your goal is, you should train them without remorse. There is nothing more manly than a bone-crushing handshake. Even if all your concern were just the size of your muscles, what a shame it would be for a big guy to have pussy hands. Besides, it is an awesome party trick to open beer with bare hands.

So what exercise to choose? There are literally thousands of grip and finger exercises. Some require a special apparatus, while others require no equipment at all. If your goal is to strengthen particularly your fingers, there is one awesome exercise for this. It requires no equipment except your bodyweight. It is called the Claw Fingertip Push-Up.

Why Not Regular Fingertip Push-Ups?
This is a good question. Let us take a look at the difference between these two exercises:

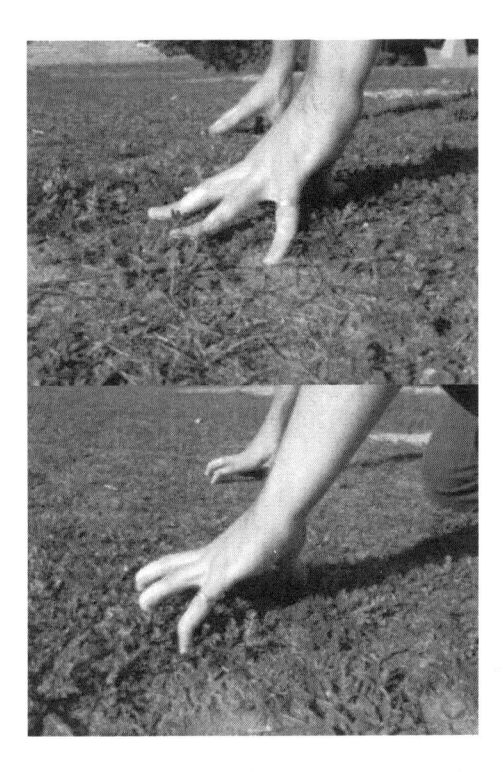

Regular Fingertip Push-Ups hand position is on the first photo and Claw Fingertip Push-Ups on the second.

As you can see, the difference is in the last fingers' joint involvement. Obviously, the claw version is harder, which is awesome. Just try it right now. Additionally, it is better for your finger joints. If you have hyperextension in them (like I do, look at the first photo), then you will feel the difference right away.

How to Perform Claw Fingertip Push-Ups?

They are very similar to ordinary push-ups, so the basic technique tips work for them also. I mean, your body should be straight, feet together or at least almost touching, and hands under your shoulders at shoulder width. As for fingers, you should literally be on the tips of your fingers. Fingers should be bent in the last joint to achieve this position. At first, it is going to hurt, but with practice, Claw Fingertip Push-Ups will become easier. One tip: you want to grab the floor with your fingers in this position. This way you will involve your fingers even more and it will strengthen your "claws".

Check these pictures out for a demonstration:

There is big possibility that you will not be able to perform Claw Fingertip Push-Ups right away. Maybe you will not be able even to hold the top position of this exercise. Do not get frustrated. Start slowly. Start with Claw Fingertip Push-Ups from your knees. If you cannot push yourself up from that position, then try just holding yourself in it. Treat this exercise as any other strength move. You do not expect to press 200 lb overhead right away, right? So do not rush things. Remember, the true master of Claw Fingertip Push-Up will have flesh-tearing "claws" and finger strength to match, but this will take lots of time and practice.

Going Beyond

Well, at some point you will find out that regular Claw Fingertip Push-Ups are not a challenge anymore. What to do then? There are several ways:

1. *Add a weighted vest.* Simple and effective. No thinking involved. If the regular version is easy, add a couple of pounds and you will have a new challenge.

2. *Start decreasing number of fingers.* If regular version is easy, try to use only 4 fingers of both hands. Then 3. Then 2. Mix them as you wish. For example, use your index finger, pinky and thumb, or middle, ring and thumb. Also, you can mix different fingers and the number of them on different hands.

3. Progress to one arm. If the regular version is easy, progress to One-Arm Claw Fingertip Push-Ups. They will be challenging.

4. Mix all of above techniques. Feel the freedom.

Closing Thoughts

Now you have the blueprint to finger strength only few people possess (if any). Strive for One-Arm One-Finger Claw Fingertip Push-Ups with weighted vest for reps and you will possess the strength not only to break a watermelon, but also to break a brick wall!

SANDBAGS

HOW TO MAKE A SANDBAG

There are two different ways to make a sandbag. Both methods begin identically. First, take a bag, preferably an army duffel one or any bag made of tight material, for example, made of canvas. It is cheap, heavy duty, and you can find something like this almost everywhere. If you are so ghetto that you find even this expensive, then you can use construction-style bags. Here in Ukraine, they cost approximately $2. To tell you the truth, my first sandbag was made of a couple of such construction-style bags, and I was not complaining.

Ok, the outer bag is now ready. The next step will be buying a couple of huge trash-bags and stuffing them inside of the outer bag. This will ensure that you will not be cleaning your home gym after every session (of course, if you train indoors), and it will cost you a couple of cents. The inner bag is ready too.

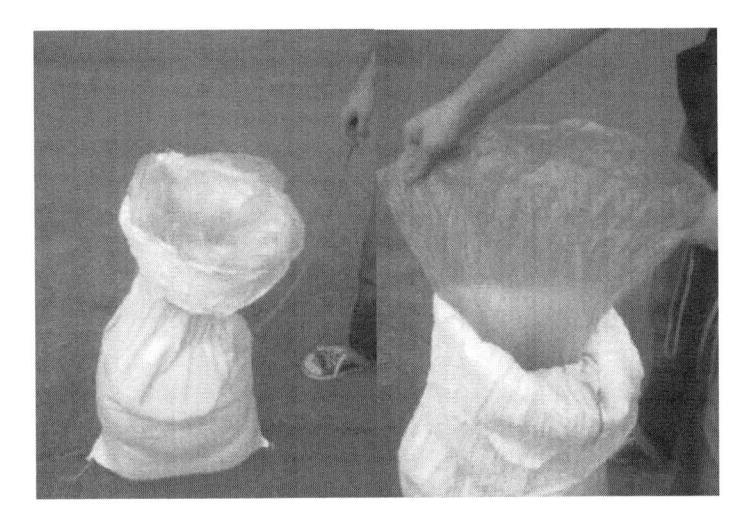

Now I will explain to you the difference between the two ways of making a sandbag.

The first one is the simplest and the least time-consuming. Get sand - stuff it inside the bag - lace it up - train! You can either buy sand, or go to the beach with a shovel and get it for free. When you put sand inside the bag, just tie it with a lace or a wire. The sandbag is ready. Weigh it if you want. You can start training. When the sandbag becomes light, add more sand inside. Pros of this method: easy, time-efficient. Cons: the sandbag will be non-adjustable, which is not so good if you plan to use one sandbag for several exercises.

Here is *the second way*, which will allow you to make your sandbag adjustable. What is the major difference? When you get the sand, you should divide it and stuff into smaller bags. They could be, for example, small trash-bags or something else of such size. After stuffing the sand inside just duct-tape them (or scotch-tape them) thickly. You don't want them to tear, right? Weigh and mark every small bag. For example, I have small bags in the following weights (in kilos): 16.5, 14, 12, 13.5, 11, 7, 5 etc.

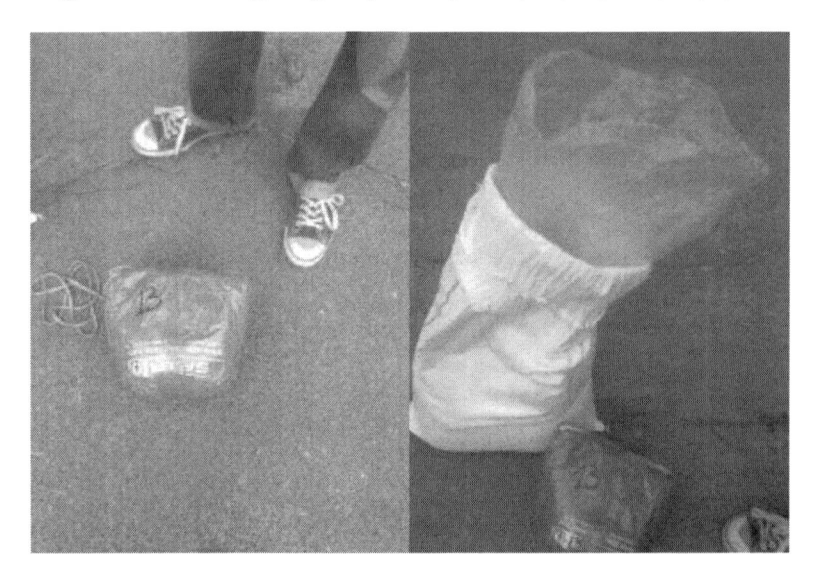

So now you can use these small bags similar to barbell plates. Just put them inside the bag and lace it. Here we go. Now you have an adjustable sandbag, which can be used effectively as a supplement to your current training implements or as an amazing standalone tool.

Some additional tips:

1. You can use any filler you want. You can try rice or cement. However, sand still remains the safest while being the heaviest. You can

drop a bag filled with sand on your feet and remain uninjured.

2. If you live in country where it snows in winter, you might want to get a little bit more sand than you need during the warm period. I live in such a climate. I went to the beach to get some sand from under the snow while it was -10C. Such an activity is definitely rough, but not for everyone.

3. If you are going to make an adjustable sandbag, try to make small bags in pairs. For example, 2.5, 2.5, 5, 5, 10, 10, etc. You will need this when you progress to advanced two-handed sandbag exercises such as the Double Sandbag Deadlift. Also, weigh your small bags precisely.

5 SANDBAG STRENGTH TRAINING BENEFITS

So I was sitting and thinking one day: "Why is sandbag strength training not really popular nowadays?" Two answers came into to my mind. Firstly, sandbag training is really tough. It is not for all those boys and girls that attend fitness clubs to get social. It is not for all those fat rich people that are so used to luxury and comfort that *drive* to a fitness club to *walk* on a treadmill. And, of course, it is not for all those close-minded pseudo-bodybuilders that think that nothing works if it's not a barbell, dumbbell or machine. Secondly, with sandbag training there is nothing to sell. Well, almost. You need just a bag and sand.

I like heavy sandbag training because it gives you a rough reality check the first time you try it. It shows you how weak you really are. That is why you need to implement it and get stronger in it. Here are five reasons you should do so:

1. Sandbag training is cheap.

Better to say that sandbag training is ridiculously cheap. Again, you will need a bag, some sand and some time to put it all together. Almost no thinking involved. My recent sandbag cost me under $5. And all I paid for was a bag. As for the sand, I made some "research" on how to get it free and decided that the most cost effective solution was to steal it from construction site near home at night. That's how we do it in Ukraine. Rough Strength style, baby! But I digress. Just count the costs. No gym memberships, no bars, no plates, no dumbbells, nothing. It is a fully equipped home gym for under $5. I think I made my point.

2. Sandbag training develops real life strength.

When I heard term "functional training" for the first time, I thought: "Wow! That is a really cool term for strength training". Later, when it became popular and fitness clubs started labeling everything as "functional", this term became not so pleasing as before. Well, I don't want to be rude, but how the fuck is a bosu-ball functional? What real life function of the body does it train? Or how are 1 kg dumbbells functional? Smart marketers are selling useless crap to dumb people. That is functional. That is why I prefer to use the term real life strength. Anyway, sandbags develop the kind of strength you can use in daily activities. Of course, I am not talking here about light weight sandbags. You will feel this benefit when you will work up in basic exercises to at least a sandbag equal to your bodyweight.

3. Sandbag training develops muscles that you were not aware of.

It is true. Just try it. You will feel soreness in muscles you would otherwise never have thought existed. Training with a sandbag forces your body to use its stabilizers MUCH more, because the bag is always uncomfortable, unstable, it is always changing its form and always trying to escape from your hands. Training with a sandbag reminds me of wrestling a human. Well, at least a dead human.

Is sandbag training optimal for building muscles (again "optimal", have you noticed?)? Well, it is hard to say. More yes than no. Lift a damn sandbag, remember about progressive resistance, eat the right diet with a slight calorie surplus, sleep, and grow. It is as simple as that. You will build a decent muscular body with strength to match.

4. Sandbag training develops bone-crushing grip.

Have you ever tried to pick up a heavy sandbag? Were you able to crush it? The answer is probably 'no'. This is because it is almost impossible to get a good grip on a sandbag. It is hard and it is uncomfortable. Your fingers will get a workout-in-a-workout. Be ready for hard work. You will be able to lift less weight than with a barbell because of this factor. However, your muscles will actually work more. Resistance is resistance. Prepare to obtain a pair of vise-grip hands.

5. You always need to lift a sandbag off the floor.

This is a big factor. People nowadays seem to be "overcomfortable" with their training. They use a treadmill over outdoor running, the Bench Press over the Military Press, and Leg Presses over Squats and Deadlifts. I can go on and on. Then they wonder why they are so fat. That's why. Do some more work. Such "overcomfort" will not work with sandbag strength training. You always need to lift a sandbag off the floor. This means more work and more fat loss. Just try it.

I hope I gave you some reasons at least to give sandbag strength training a shot. It is definitely not for everybody. Just for the toughest of us.

SANDBAG SHOULDERING

If I were on uninhabited island and doomed to do only one exercise, it definitely would be the Deadlift (well, maybe the Handstand Push-Up, but let us stick to the Deadlift, because the awesome intro for the article otherwise will fall apart). Its results are proven over centuries and it has the most impact on muscle building and overall strength gains. Of course, I would also choose it because it is one of my favorite exercises. However, there is one little problem. As a rule, there are no barbells and plates on islands. There is only sand and, if you are lucky, a thick-cloth bag around. No big deal. Shoulder it!

Shouldering is as old as sandbags are. Old-time strongmen used to shoulder great poundage in order to build tremendous strength. The strongest of them could shoulder 100 kg (225 lb) sandbag with one arm! I doubt that there are any men today who can replicate this feat of strength. Sandbag Shouldering is a lost feat of strength, but it is definitely worth bringing back.

Sandbag Shouldering is a simple exercise. You literally lift the sandbag off the floor and up to the shoulder. There is no hidden context, but let me warn you, do not be fooled by its simplicity. It is hard as hell when done with decent poundage. It is a test of willpower when done for high reps. Those who say that Sandbag Shouldering is easy definitely have not done it heavy and/or for high reps.

Shouldering is a full-body exercise. The main muscle groups that perform the action are lower back, hips, hamstrings, forearms, biceps, upper back, shoulders, pectorals, calves and quads. As you can see, Sandbag Shouldering covers almost every area of the body. The only muscle group that stays not fully involved is triceps. More on that later. The exercise mechanics are similar to the Deadlift and the Power Clean. However, Shouldering requires less weight than the Deadlift and involves all muscle groups in a less static and more dynamic manner, which is excellent for MMA fighters by the way. It is also less technically demanding than the Power Clean. The whole movement is performed like this:

1. Deadlift the weight off the floor.

2. High-pull it, and bear-hug it under.

3. Jump with it.

4. Clean it to the shoulder.

It is very important to keep your lower back as straight as possible throughout the movement. To get this done you need to look a bit up and imagine that you are arching your back.

This variation of Sandbag Shouldering is the most powerful. It will allow you to use the heaviest weight with good form. You can watch some videos on YouTube where guys do shouldering another way with the bag too far from the body and in one movement. Believe me, those guys are not even close to using heavy poundage. I mean HEAVY! As we all know, the heavier the bag, the more muscle you can build.

If you are serious about getting as strong as possible, it will be a good idea to incorporate Sandbag Shouldering into your routine. It should be used in place of the row/lower body pull. For example, you can incorporate shouldering in your full-body routine like this:

A1) Front Squat 5x5
A2) Floor Press 5x5
A3) Shouldering 5x2

Perform all the exercises in circuit fashion, one-by-one. Rest as much as needed between exercises, but not more than 5 minutes. Feel free to add some core or arm work after all the circuits are done if you dare, but no more than one exercise and no more than 2 sets of 5-10 reps.

Here you go. Now you have everything you need to start reaping the benefits of heavy Sandbag Shouldering. However, there is a little bonus for you.

Everybody knows the 20-rep Squat routine and some know the 20-rep Deadlift routine. There is no doubt that these programs helped pack on a lot of mass, and ordinary guys became extraordinary walls of muscle as a result. So here is the Rough Strength Solution for those of you who accept the challenge:

20-Rep Sandbag Shouldering Routine

It is bloody mess. I dare those of you who are brave enough to try this routine. You will have the most brutal experience in your life. So here it is:

A) Upper-Body Push 3x5
B1) Sandbag Shouldering 1x20
B2) Light Pullovers (or Rader Chest Pull) 1x20

Rest as much as needed. No need to bother with rep speed. Progression will be conventional. Once you get all the reps, put more sand inside the bag and/or increase the weight for upper-body push movements. You can choose any upper-body push you want: Military Press, Floor Press, Bench Press, and Weighted Dips - pick one or couple. You can even pick three and rotate them every training session. It can look something like this:

Monday - Military Press
Wednesday - Floor Press
Friday - Weighted Dips

To say that the Shouldering will be brutal is to say nothing. Choose HEAVY weight if you want to reap the benefits. Rep 5 will be hard. Rep 10 will seem like the end of the set, but your goal is twenty. Remember that and make it to that point. Then immediately perform the set of Breathing Pullovers or Rader Chest Pulls. If you have done everything as outlined here, you will not have desire to do any isolation work. If not, then you probably were not shouldering heavy enough.

The next point is workout frequency. Try 3 full-body workouts per week. If you feel that your recovery is impaired, then try 2 full-body workouts per week.

Your nutrition and rest should be in check also. Consume enough calories. Drink a gallon of milk a day as old-timers said (of course, only if you have very fast metabolism and it's hard for you to gain any weight; if that's not the case, then study the "Nutrition" section precisely). It is mandatory to sleep at least 8 hours at night (the more the better), and to have a 20-30 minute nap during the day.

These are all the tips. Do not overcomplicate things! Keep it simple and it WILL be effective. Be ready to purchase new clothes.

HOW TO DOMINATE THE SANDBAG ZERCHER SQUAT

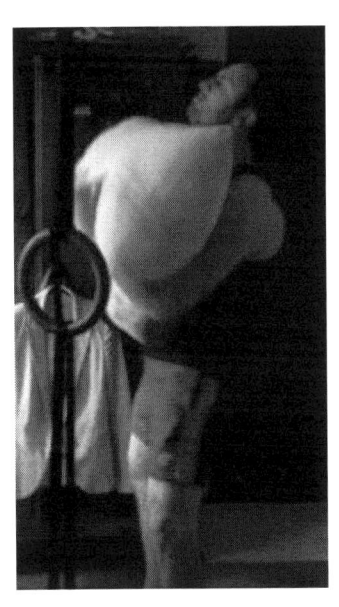

I was a little nervous before the set. Still it was an increase in working weight; it was unknown ground. The heavy sandbag was lying silently in front of me, challenging me to lift it up with all its appearance. The set was going to be filmed, so I had no chance to screw up. I stood above the bag showing my domination and closed my eyes to visualize inevitable victory. I quietly squatted down and grabbed the sides of the enemy. Next thing I deadlifted the bag with rage and jumped explosively to catch it in the Zercher position. My goal was at least 3 reps. It's all probably because of adrenaline running through my veins, but when I reached the goal I still felt energy and nailed 2 more. It was really hard to put this bastard down quietly, but I did my best and finally got the feeling of euphoria of a new PR mixed with faintness. My goal of doing a 90 kg Sandbag Zercher Squat was one step closer.

As you probably noticed, this article is about sandbag strength training, specifically Sandbag Zercher Squat. Above you have read my literary attempt to explain how I was able to nail 85 kg for 5 reps in this exercise. It was filmed and you can watch the video here [13]. Of course, I can see some flaws in form, but no PR was set with perfect technique.

Anyway, the goal of this article is to explain what kind of beast the Sandbag Zercher Squat is, and importantly, why you need to dominate it. Let's go.

Enter the Sandbag Zercher Squat

The Sandbag Zercher Squat [SZS] is a variation of basic squat exercise. Every living person (and probably some dead) should be practicing some sort of squatting regularly. There are plenty of reasons why you need to perform it. Increased leg strength, increased sprinting speed, a higher vertical jump, a more functional body, better sports performance – to name just few. Besides, the bottom position of the squat is essential for human beings. The ability to sit in a full squat position means that your ankle flexibility is optimal. I was really surprised how many people cannot perform such simple feat due to their poor flexibility.

What is the difference between SZS and regular Barbell Squat? I will provide the answer:

- In a Barbell Squat, we take barbell from squat stands or a power rack. Then we take couple of steps back and perform the reps. *In the SZS, we take a sandbag off the floor.* So we need to deadlift the bag with a high pull first, then jump with it, and clean it to a Zercher position *[the Zercher position is a place between your forearms and upper arms, on the other side of the elbow. The Zercher Squat was created and popularized by Ed Zercher, a strongman from the 1930s].* Only after that we are able to perform the reps. Obviously, there is much more auxiliary work with SZS. This means several things that will be explained below.

- In a Barbell Squat, you work against the resistance on your back. *In SZS, you work against resistance in front of you.* Besides, holding a sandbag in a Zercher position involves your biceps into action big time.

- *The range of motion in a SZS is shorter than in Barbell Squat.* You are holding the bag in front of you and can squat down only until your arms touch your legs. You can definitely squat lower with a barbell.

- *The Barbell Squat feels much more comfortable than the SZS.* A sandbag is odd and awkward, which makes it more interesting and somewhat more beneficial to train with.

Why Do You Need the SZS?

You should clearly understand the pros and cons of the Sandbag Zercher Squat to decide whether you need it in your program or not.

Pros:

- More calorie expenditure. This means that you can achieve more fat loss if your diet is proper.

- Working against resistance in front of you teaches you to fight the force, again, in front of you. This is beneficial for strongmen, football, hockey players, wrestlers, and MMA fighters. They all deal with resistance in front of them most of the time.

- A sandbag is awkward, so it will develop your stabilizer muscles much more.

- The SZS builds grip strength. You need to crush the bag hard during the clean.
- Sandbag training is minimalistic and cheap, as well as tough and badass.
- Masters of the SZS will possess tremendous full-body strength.

Cons:

- It is hard to progress in SZS if it is combined with upper body pulling/rowing exercises. It is because of huge biceps involvement.
- It is not optimal for leg size. Leg muscle activation is poor compared to Barbell Squats.
- It is hard. Very few people will withstand the demand of the exercise.

Now you can decide whether you need to bother and become cooler or just remain girly and weak.

Why Do I Train the SZS?

This question is easy to answer. Firstly, I always practice what I preach. It is a never-ending exploration of the Rough Strength Method with its limitless possibilities. Secondly, legs are not my primary focus. I am not a bodybuilder. As long as the SZS allows me to get stronger and develop better coordination as well as agility, the benefits of the exercise are far more outstanding than its restrictions. This exercise definitely teaches you right things.

How to Perform the SZS Correctly?

Let us get to the main part. What are the main technique points? Let's see:

1. Put the sandbag in front of you. It should be between your legs.

2. Lean forward and squat just like in the deadlift position. Keep your lower back arched. If you see yourself from the side, your butt should be lower than your shoulders and higher than your knees. Just look at the picture above.

3. Crush the sides of the sandbag.

4. Deadlift the sandbag off the floor just past the knee level, and explosively drive your hips forward and shrug your shoulders pulling the bag up with intention to jump. You should be able to catch it in Zercher position. Watch the video at the beginning of the article for reference, or study this video of Power Clean [14].

5. Re-catch the bag if needed.

6. Squat down until your arms touch your legs. Stand up and repeat for the desired number of reps. *The best advice I got on squat technique was not to think about standing up but rather about pushing the ground away through my heels.* In my experience, this little tweak cleans up everybody's squat technique the first time the person tries it.

7. Lower the sandbag down slowly and with respect.

These are the basic technique points you need to address to learn proper form of the Sandbag Zercher Squat. Now we move on to get to programming.

How to Incorporate the SZS into Your Program?

We finally get to the juicy part. How to really dominate the Sandbag Zercher Squat? As always, programming requires an individual approach. I divided people who might possibly be interested in the SZS into 5 categories: novice trainees, bodybuilders, powerlifters, Rough Strength Method followers, and others. We shall examine how each group can incorporate the SZS into their programs:

Novice Trainees

First of all, I will talk about novice trainees that want to explore the benefits of the Sandbag Zercher Squat. Who do I consider a novice? People that are training seriously, consistently, and effectively less than 2 years. People that were wasting time in the gym for 5, 10, 15 or whatever years, and are just starting proper strength training are also considered novices. What should you know about novice training methods? All they need is to get stronger. What is important is the fact that the SZS is not that demanding in this phase, which is why you can use it in a full-body workout with success. Here is an example:

A1) Dips 3 x 5 with 7 rep maximum [RM]
A2) Pull-Ups 3 x 5 with 7 RM
B) Sandbag Zercher Squats 3 x 5 with 7 RM

Perform the first two exercises alternating the sets of each. Rest between sets for no more than 2 minutes. 7 RM means the weight you can lift for maximum of 7 repetitions.

Your arms will be tired after upper body work, but you probably will not be able to notice it in the performance of the SZS.

Bodybuilders

If you chose the bodybuilder's path, then the SZS is not optimal for you. If you want to try something new and spicy, here is an example leg workout for you:

A) Sandbag Zercher Squats 3 x 6-8
B) Barbell Lunges 3 x 10-12 (per leg)
C) Romanian Deadlifts 3-4 x 10-12
D) One-Leg Calf Raises 3-4 x 15-20

Pick a weight that feels comfortable, but not light, and allows you to feel the target muscles. Perform all exercises in a straight fashion, one after another. Rest no more than 1-2 minutes between sets and no more than 3-5 minutes between exercises.

Why is the SZS is the first exercise? It is the most demanding of them all. If you put it in the end, you will not be able to accomplish much. Here is another example of a bodybuilder's workout. This time it would be Legs/Arms:

A) Sandbag Zercher Squats 3 x 6-8
B) One-Leg Deadlifts 3 x 10-12 (each leg)
C) Towel One-Arm Curls 3 x 10-12 (each arm)
D) Lying Triceps Extensions 3-4 x 10-12

Recommendations on working weight and rest are the same as above.

Again, the SZS should be first in this kind of workout. Your biceps would be blasted after them so I decided to put Towel Curls here to make it even spicier. Why not a full-body workout? For experienced bodybuilders splits are more suitable, in my opinion.

Powerlifters

If you are into this powerlifting thing, then obviously you should use the SZS as auxiliary work after your Squat or Deadlift workout. Depending on your program, there are several ways to incorporate this exercise. Again, as with bodybuilders, it is probably not the best option (Zercher Good Mornings would be more suitable). I will assume that you want to add the SZS as assistance work after your max effort squat session. The workout can look like this:

A) Barbell Squats – work up to 3 RM
B1) Sandbag Zercher Squats 4 x 8
B2) Barbell Good Mornings 4 x 10

Everything is clear with the squat. Work up to a weight you can squat only for 3 reps. For assistance work pick a weight that is comfortable.

Rough Strength Method followers (Strongmen included)
Finally, Rough Strength disciples. With an increase in working weight, you will need to isolate the SZS from any upper body work if your goal is to get stronger in this exercise. I used an Upper Body – Lower Body – Upper Body split with success for this goal. So my lower body session looked something like this:

A) Sandbag Zercher Squats 3 x 5 with 7RM
B) Sandbag Shouldering 5 x 1 (each side, so it's 10 sets total)
C) Pistols 3 x 10-12 (bodyweight, optional)
D) One-Leg Calf Raises with bodyweight 3 x 25 (controlled, with a squeeze at the top, 2 seconds up, 2 seconds hold at the top and 2 seconds down)

Sometimes I did not have much time, so I trained the SZS solely because it is the exercise I want to improve most out of those four.

There are lots of variation options here. For example, you can substitute Sandbag Shouldering with Sandbag Bear Hug Good Mornings or Glute Ham Raises. If you prefer to concentrate on Pistols, you can put them first and add weight to them. To make it work you should put the SZS later and add more reps while cutting the working weight. The variations are endless, and your fantasy is the limit.

Others
Do not be fooled by the "Others" label. This group contains a quite badass category of people. I will put in here MMA fighters, crossfitters, football, hockey players, wrestlers, and other functional athletes. You could also add military men, firefighters and other professions that require stamina in addition to strength. What can their conditioning workout look like?

A1) Clap Push-Ups for 10 reps
A2) Pull-Ups for 10 reps
A3) Sandbag Zercher Squat for 10 reps
A4) Kettlebell Double Swings for 10 reps

A5) Medball Throws with partner for 10 throws

Perform all the exercises one by one with as little rest as possible. Start with 3 circuits and work up to 5 circuits with no rest between exercises. Rest for 1-2 minutes between circuits. This will build unstoppable stamina and conditioning.

Closing Thoughts

The Sandbag Zercher Squat is an exercise that brings results. It is hard. Most people will find it uncomfortable. Some people will find it impossible to perform on a regular basis. Torn fingers, annoying soreness in biceps, a strong desire to puke right in the middle of the set – that is what is waiting for you. Is it worth it? Hell yes.

KETTLEBELLS

THE 5 KEYS TO DOUBLE KETTLEBELL TRAINING

Kettlebells are unquestionably one of the most versatile, functional, and fun training tools out there. When it comes to kettlebell training, two is better than one in most cases. "Double gun = double fun", to quote the classics if I may. To get a better understanding of, and to avoid any misconceptions about how to properly use double kettlebells, let us breakdown the benefits of double kettlebell training:

Benefits of Double Kettlebell Training

- *Double kettlebell exercises are better for overall strength.* For example, if we perform the Double Kettlebell Military Press with two 32 kg kettlebells, that is 64 kg of overall intensity. It is much harder to find a person that will be able to press 64 kg with one arm for single than the one who can lift two 32 kg kettlebells for 5-10 reps despite the same total weight.

- *Double kettlebell training is better for hypertrophy.* More overall intensity results in more training volume, which, if applied correctly and with a proper diet, leads to more muscle gains. You know, that good old saying "heavy weight for high reps".

- *Double kettlebell training is much more badass.* One of the manliest exercises on Earth, in my opinion, is the Double Kettlebell Snatch (with 32 kg kettlebells or heavier, of course).

Ok, so now you know why double kettlebell training is awesome. What is next?

Tips to Training with Two Kettlebells

1) Remember that you are training with TWO kettlebells. It is always tempting to add weight when you finally reached your desired repetition goal, but it is not that simple with kettlebells. It is not a barbell with lots of possible small increments. Remember that when you make a jump from 32kg kettlebells to

36kg, it is not just 4kg, but actually it is 8 kg total. This is pretty decent by any means. If you are squeezing 3 sets of 5 reps with 32kg, there is a high possibility that you will need to work on singles with 36kg.

The take-home point: take your time and master the weight fully before progressing forward.

2) Learn the Double Kettlebell Clean Exercise. It may seem obvious, but this is quite important tip. Just look at most exercises; they all require you to clean the kettlebells before performing the movement. In a perfect scenario, you should not even feel the clean. So, if you are just starting with double kettlebell training, my advice would be to learn proper clean technique as soon as possible.

3) If you struggle to synchronize the kettlebells throughout the movement, imagine that it is a barbell. This is quite interesting tip. I successfully used it many times with clients that are just getting used to double kettlebell training. As soon as they imagined that their hands resisted against something solid instead of two unlinked objects, they started to move kettlebells through space simultaneously.

4) If you struggle to move to heavier kettlebells, just progress to harder exercises instead. This unconventional approach to "progressive resistance" principle was taken, I guess, from bodyweight strength training. For example, if you can perform Double Kettlebell Military Presses with 32kg, but 36kg seems impossible for some reason, instead of crying in the bathroom and blaming the government, you can progress to a harder exercise with the same 32kg kettlebells. For example, your progression can be the Double Military Press to the One-Arm Seated Overhead Press on the floor (Double Seated Press on the floor can lead to kettlebell stuck in your head due to falling on your back; however, using it or not is solely your decision). Then from that to the Double Sots Press, which is an overhead press from a full squat.

5) Strive to learn the Double Kettlebell Snatch. One reason: because it is awesome. With all seriousness, it is the most technically demanding lift with two kettlebells and it pays off. I advise you find a good trainer to show you how to perform this complex movement. Once you get it down, you will see huge gains in strength and conditioning.

Closing Thoughts

In the end, I should warn you: if you have not tried it, you risk getting totally hooked. Be ready to quit your job and drop your life to get another dose of this drug called "Kettlebell".

HOW TO MAKE YOUR KETTLEBELLS HEAVIER

The kettlebell is one of the best implements out there when we are talking about gaining strength, building muscle, getting lean and attaining superhuman endurance. No matter what your goal is, you can benefit from kettlebell training big time. Besides, this tool is the least space consuming (after your bodyweight, of course). You can even use kettlebells as part of your room decoration.

As you probably know, the heavier the kettlebell you use, the more benefits you will reap. A heavier kettlebell = more strength, more muscle, more fat loss. Therefore, you always need to aim to lift bells that are more challenging. If your weight is 80 kg and more, then you will need a pair of 40 kg, 44 kg and maybe even 48 kg bells. For example, Double Front Squat with a pair of 32 kg kettlebells became ridiculously easy for me very quickly at the weight of 80 kg. Heck, squatting with 40 kg kettlebells is not a problem anymore.

However, there is one nuance with kettlebells. They are quite expensive. You probably will not be able to afford buying a new pair of kettlebells every time you hit PRs. No problem. Kettlebells offer different kinds of progressions to master the weight. If your Military Press becomes too easy, try Seated Press. If Seated Presses also become easy, then try the Sots Press. In fact, you can vary not only exercises. You can cut rest periods between sets (which is also great for fat loss), shift lifting tempo, go for high reps, add sets, etc. What if all that becomes easy, too? You need to buy a new pair.

Here is the thing though. For example, your 32 kg kettlebells became as light for you as air through all those progressions I mentioned above. No need to buy 36 kg ones. You can skip them and purchase 40s. What to do if you cannot lift 40 kg bells right away? Take your time. Do not rush things. Finally, we have reached the main topic of this article.

Rough Strength Solution for Making Your Kettlebells Heavier

Firstly, the disclaimer. The technique that I am going to reveal is dangerous if done improperly. Try it at your own risk. I am not responsible in any manner whatsoever for any injury which may occur through reading and following the instructions herein.

Secondly, I really **do not recommend** using this stuff in ballistic exercises, especially the Double Snatch. You can use it only in conventional movements like Presses, Rows, Squats and Deadlifts for added resistance.

So here is the fun part. You have a kettlebell and the desire to make it heavier. There are several options:

1. Kettlebell, dumbbell, and rope

All you need are a kettlebell, a dumbbell, and some rope. You can attach the dumbbell to the kettlebell's handle with a knot and rope it to the other side of the handle. Finish it with a double knot under the dumbbell. Now everything is set. Look at photos.

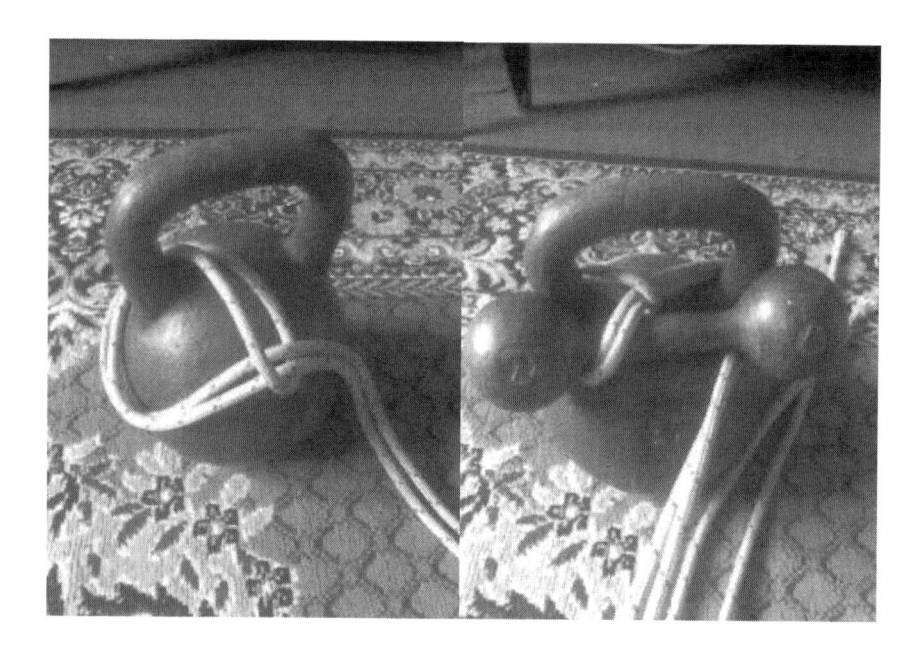

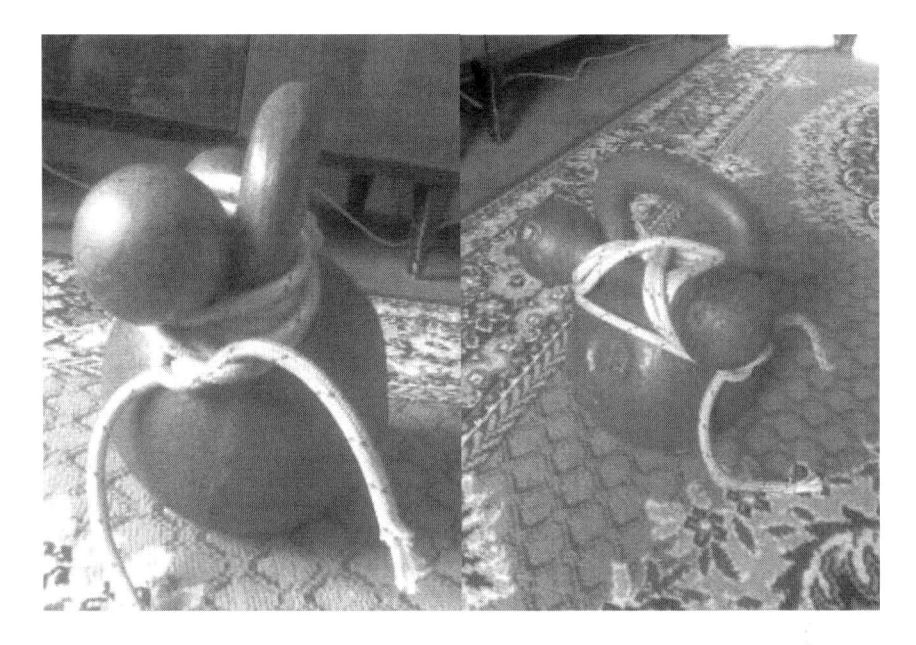

Here is a 32 kg kettlebell and a 4 kg dumbbell attached to it. The 36 kg kettlebell is ready. You will need a good rope for this. Additionally, do not forget to check all the knots before training. They should hold dumbbell very tight. This setup seems a bit time consuming, but who cares? You need results, right?

2. Kettlebell and Chains

The second option is to attach chains to your kettlebell. This method is less useful in my opinion because chains are very space consuming for their weight. In other words, there will be less space for your hand in the handle. Nevertheless, chains can offer you added resistance, which is great.

Kettlebell and Dumbbells - Part 2

I learned this awesome method from my fellow countryman and kettlebell brother Yahont.

What you need to do is to attach a heavy-duty rope or lace to the dumbbell at the right length, and just hang it on the handle of the kettlebell.

Watch this video – [15]. What he does is simple and effective.

Closing Thoughts

You can use practically everything you want for added resistance, but remember:

1. Check all the attachments before training.
2. Don't use this technique for ballistic moves.

This technique has its own flaws, but I have used it with success in my training. Of course, you miss some fun from not doing ballistic exercises with such kettlebells, but dumbbells, ropes and chains cost way less than a new pair of kettlebells.

ROUTINES

MIXING TRAINING IMPLEMENTS FOR ULTIMATE RESULTS

There are so many debates on what implement is the ultimate training tool. Barbells? Dumbbells? Sandbags? Kettlebells? Bodyweight? You name it. People tend to oppose them to each other. One camp says: "Barbells are the best because you can always make micro adjustments in weight". Others reply: "Sandbags or kegs are the best because they rock stabilizers big time; barbells cannot offer this". The third group of dudes say: "Kettlebells are the best because they are fun and versatile and can offer unique exercises". The fourth camp states: "Forget about weights! Old school bodyweight strength training is the king because you learn to master your own bodyweight".

So who is right and where is the truth?

The Truth

The truth, as always, lies somewhere in the middle. The key problem in this discussion is that people oppose all training implements to each other. People think that they have found a 'magic pill' in the form of one of them. I mean something like "Wow! Kettlebells are so fun and they take much less space than barbells. The whole Eastern Europe trains with this secret implement. That must be the end-all be-all training tool. I should drop barbell training because it's useless compared to kettlebells". This is a wrong standpoint. Every training tool has its own benefits, as well as flaws. You should understand that there is no magic training tool. Every one of them has its pros and cons.

Some Example Pros and Cons
Barbells
Pros:

- Ultimately adjustable – You can make the smallest increases in working weight. Let us assume that you can press 200 lb, but cannot nail 210 yet. With barbells, the solution can be as simple as adding 5 lb instead of 10.

- Universal – The range of exercises that can be done with a barbell is amazing. You can work your body from every angle only with a barbell and a set of plates.

- You can go maximally heavy – any other implement I tried requires less weight because of instability.

Cons:

- Very space consuming – of course, it is less space consuming than all those crappy machines in commercial gyms, but we do not take them into account. You need a solid piece of space to store a full barbell set or you need to go to those shitty fitness clubs, which is not an optimal way to train, in my opinion. You also need to remember that you may need a power rack for safety reasons.

- Expensive – A high-quality barbell and all the plates will cost you pretty decent money.

- Sometimes it works your body in unnatural angles – what can lead to injury. It is common in older athletes to drop barbell training because of shoulder or knee injuries. You can get away with many mistakes when you are young, but as you become older, you will pay your dues.

Sandbags
Pros:

- Adjustable – You can make any sandbag adjustable.

- Works stabilizers – You need serious strength to stabilize a heavy sandbag. It always changes its form.

- Works grip – Even grabbing a sandbag is a big deal.

- Increased metabolic efficiency – You will be huffing-n-puffing on any sandbag exercise. No need for cardio.

- Low price – It is almost free.

- Very safe – As long as you use sand for a filler. Drop it on your leg and feel almost nothing compared to a dumbbell or kettlebell.

Cons:

- Too much setup for some exercises – It is not a con for me, but for some people it is. Getting a sandbag in position for a Sandbag Floor Press is a workout-in-a-workout.

- You cannot adjust a sandbag quickly.

- You need to switch sides – Distribution of sand is not equal inside the sandbag.

- It can get very messy if you do not use an inner bag.

Kettlebells
Pros:
- Low space requirement – One pair of kettlebells can take up less space than a dog.
- They are versatile and fun.
- Unique movement patterns – Kettlebells offer ballistic exercises such as Swings and Snatches.
- They feel heavier – It is due to the off-axis center of mass. You will need to fight every inch of movement.
- Probably the ultimate shoulder developer.
- Very hard to break.

Cons:
- Pricey – One set of kettlebells is not so expensive, but what to do when you need to move to heavier ones?
- Leg work is pretty questionable. Especially comparing to barbells.
- Not adjustable – Either lift or go home.

Bodyweight Training
Pros:
- Requires no equipment – Hell yeah!
- Easier on joints – No external load is used. Some people would disagree with this point, but I started feeling MUCH less pain in my joints after switching my upper body work almost exclusively to calisthenics. And, yes, I do train Planche and Front Lever.
- Lightning fast strength gains – I'm talking about quicker neural adaptation here.
- You master your bodyweight – It is hard to explain this point to someone that has not felt that. Once you become somewhat proficient with your bodyweight, you will understand what I am talking about.

Cons:
- Resistance is limited to your bodyweight – It is not actually a con, but for skinny guys who try to gain mass it is. My professional advice is to start eating big! If you are on the right bodyweight program and not gaining mass, you eat too little.
- Leg work is limited.

You get the idea.

What to choose?
You will not believe me, but choose what you like and what fits your goals and conditions. Actually, the more variety there is in your training tools – the better! You can pick one or all of them. Why restrict yourself to

using only one implement if you like several? The more implements you pick – the more overall development you can expect.

You should understand that if you are a competing athlete, for example in powerlifting or weightlifting, your basic tool is the barbell. This means that most of the time you should train with it. However, adding sandbags, kettlebells, and bodyweight to the mix is worth bothering with because you can expect more overall strength. On the other hand, if you are just an average Joe who wants to be in shape and do not have the money and time to go to the gym or buy expensive equipment, it is no big deal. Bodyweight strength training will cost you nothing and you can do it anytime, anywhere. Most importantly, it brings results.

OK. So How Can I Mix All This?

The options are endless. There is a big chance that you can come up with a totally unique routine. For example, if you can go to the gym only 2 days a week you can organize the routine that will include two days of barbell training and one day of sandbag and/or bodyweight training. Here is an example schedule:

Monday – Gym
A1) Barbell Military Press 5×5
A2) Barbell Bent-Over Row 5×5

Perform all sets in an alternating fashion. Rest no more than 2 minutes between sets. Start with your seven-rep max. Use the same weight for all sets. When you will be able to finish all sets and all reps, add weight or cut the rest periods. Finish all the sets and then move on to the next exercise.

B) Barbell Squat 5×5

Rest no more than 2 minutes between sets. Start with your seven-rep max. Use the same weight for all sets. When you will be able to finish all sets and all reps, add weight or cut the rest periods.

Wednesday – Home
A1) Dips 5×5
A2) Pull-Ups 5×5
A3) Sandbag Zercher Squats 5×5

Perform all sets in circuit fashion. Rest no more than 3 minutes between sets. Start with your seven-rep max. Use the same weight for all sets. When you will be able to finish all sets and all reps, add weight, reps or cut the rest periods.

Friday – Gym
A1) Barbell Bench Press 5×5
A2) Barbell High Pull 5×5

Perform all sets in alternating fashion. Rest no more than 2 minutes between sets. Start with your seven-rep max. Use the same weight for all sets. When you will be able to finish all sets and all reps, add weight or cut the rest periods. Finish all the sets and then move on to the next exercise.

B) Barbell Lunges 5×5 (each side)

Rest no more than 2 minutes between sets. Start with your seven-rep max. Use the same weight for all sets. When you will be able to finish all sets and all reps, add weight or cut the rest periods.

Also, if you want, you can mix everything in a crazy unique strength building routine. It may look something like this:

Monday

A1) Handstand Push-Ups 8×3
A2) Barbell Bent-Over Row 8×3
A3) Sandbag Zercher Squats 8×3

Perform all sets in circuit fashion. Rest no more than 2 minutes between sets. Start with your seven-rep max. Use the same weight for all sets. When you will be able to finish all sets and all reps, add weight, reps or cut the rest periods.

Wednesday

A1) Barbell Floor Press 5×5
A2) Weighted Pull-Ups 5×5
A3) Kettlebell Double Snatch 5×5

Perform all sets in circuit fashion. Rest no more than 3 minutes between sets. Start with your seven-rep max. Use the same weight for all sets. When you will be able to finish all sets and all reps, add weight, reps, or cut the rest periods.

Friday

A1) Kettlebell One-Arm Military Press 4×6
A2) Sandbag Shouldering 4×3 (each side)
A3) Barbell Squat 4×6

Perform all sets in circuit fashion. Rest no more than 3 minutes between sets. Start with your eight-rep max. Use the same weight for all sets. When you will be able to finish all sets and all reps, add weight, reps or cut the rest periods.

I used Monday/Wednesday/Friday only for example purposes. Pick the days that fit you. Use one of the above routines and drop me a note on how it worked. Check out "About the Author" section for contact information.

In conclusion, I would like to say some words on being open-minded.

Do not be afraid to go against what society, your friends, or the media tells you. Try different implements and discover what works for you. Mix what you like and reap tremendous benefits.

TOP 3 STRENGTH ROUTINES FOR BEGINNERS

"What routine is the best?"
"What routine will build muscle?"
"What routine will build strength?"

I get these questions all the time. Firstly, there is no such thing as "the best routine". For beginners, the best routine is the one you stick to for a long enough time to get results.

Secondly, everyone is different. Working as a trainer, I see this constantly. People find crappy programs on the internet and follow them blindly in hope of results. Most of the time they fail miserably because generic programs do not work. They do not take into account your biomechanics, your conditions, your performance capacity etc. You should understand that the only program that will work for you is a **personalized one**, tailored to your current goals and circumstances. So programs available on the internet should be considered as templates, rather than actual training routines.

Nevertheless, there are three reasonable famous programs that will work for beginners no matter what their conditions are. I would like to share them with you in this article, as well as give you Rough Strength versions of them.

Mark Rippetoe's Starting Strength
Original version:
Workout A
1) Barbell Squat 3 x 5
2) Barbell Bench Press 3 x 5
3) Barbell Deadlift 1 x 5

Workout B
1) Barbell Squat 3 x 5
2) Barbell Military Press 3 x 5
3) Barbell Power Clean 5 x 3

Workouts A and B should be alternated on a 3-times-per-week basis. For example, Monday – workout A, Wednesday – workout B, Friday – workout A, Monday – workout B etc.

Rough Strength version:
Workout A
1) Sandbag Zercher Squats 3 x 5
2) Weighted Push-Ups 3 x 5
3) Kettlebell Double Swings 3 x 5

Workout B
1) Sandbag Bear Hug Squats 3 x 5
2) Handstand Push-Ups 3 x 5
3) Sandbag Shouldering 5 x 3

Same rules as above.

My comments:
I mentioned the Starting Strength routine in "How to Gain Strength" article for a good reason. This program has proven its usefulness with lots of trainees. It helped many people that were just a step away from quitting. In my experience, this might be the most effective template for beginners. It worked like a clock for me and my clients. Its beauty is in its simplicity and minimalism. There is nothing unnecessary, and that is why it works. The only downside is that Power Cleans are quite technically demanding. However, you can change it to weighted chin-ups if you like.

Iron Addict's SPBR
Original version:
Monday
Squat or box squat 2-3 x 5
Glute/Ham Raises or pullthroughs 3 x 10
Bent Row or Chest Supported row 4 x 6
Barbell or Dumbbell Curl 3 x 8
Calf Raises 3 x 15

Wednesday
Bench Press or low board press 3 x 5, or 3 x 3
Incline Dumbbell Bench Press 4 x 8
Military or Dumbbell Shoulder Press 3 x 8
Skull Crushers 3 x 10
Ab work 3 x 10

Friday
Deadlift or rack deadlift 2-3 x 5
Leg press 2 x 10
Chin or lat pull-down 4 x 6
Barbell or Dumbbell Curl 3 x 8
Calf Raises 3 x 15

Monday
Incline bench press or Incline Dumbbell Press 3 x 5, or 3 x 3
Dumbbell Bench Press 4 x 8
Military or Dumbbell Shoulder Press 3 x 8
Tricep pushdowns 3 x 10
Ab work 3 x 10

Wednesday
Repeat

Rough Strength version:
Monday
Sandbag Zercher Squat 2-3 x 5
Glute/Ham Raises 3 x 10
Kettlebell Double Bent Row 4 x 6
One-Arm Towel Curl 3 x 8
Calf Raises 3 x 15

Wednesday
Sandbag Floor Press 3 x 5, or 3 x 3
Incline Kettlebell Bench Press 4 x 8
One-Arm Kettlebell Military Press 3 x 8
Sandbag Skull Crushers 3 x 10
Ab work 3 x 10

Friday
Kettlebell One-Arm Snatch 2-3 x 5
Kettlebell Double Front Squat 2 x 10
Chin-Ups 4 x 6
Sandbag Curl 3 x 8
Calf Raises 3 x 15

Monday
Handstand Push-Ups 3 x 5, or 3 x 3
Kettlebell Floor Press 4 x 8
Sandbag Shoulder Press 3 x 8
Incline Tiger Bend Push-Ups 3 x 10
Ab work 3 x 10

Wednesday
Repeat

My comments:
This routine is simply awesome. It gives you enough variety and options, while having a solid base. It combines strength work and volume – the best of both worlds. Most of trainees should progress very well on it. The only downside of this routine is that it stops working someday, but it could be more than 6 months of steady progress.

Pavel Tsatsouline's Power to the People
Original version:
1) Barbell Side Press 2 x 5
2) Barbell Deadlift 2 x 5
Monday through Friday – workout days. Weekend – rest. First set is approximately 5-rep maximum. Second set is 90% of the first one. Plain and simple.

Rough Strength version:
1) Kettlebell Side Press 2 x 5
2) Sandbag Zercher Squat 2 x 5
Same as above.

My comments:
It is highly unlikely that you will build a lot of muscle using this routine, but you will gain a lot of strength, which is all that matters, right? It is simple and hard to screw up, but definitely not easy. The only downside is that your workouts will take probably less than 30 minutes and you will not be able to make an excuse that you have no time.

Closing Thoughts

There you have it. These are my top three routines for building strength for beginners. Do not be afraid of "beginner" status. In any case, if you cannot do double bodyweight Deadlifts for reps, then you definitely can benefit from these routines. If you can, you still should test these routines for variety.

5 X 5 STRENGTH TRAINING TEMPLATE: HOW TO DO IT RIGHT

So this is another article on basics, specifically on the 5 x 5 strength template. I really like this approach, and I am always amazed how it always gets lost and returns.

At first, let us take a look at the common variations of this famous training template.

5 x 5 Strength Training Template in History and Its Variations

Well, I do not really know whether old-timers used exactly 5 sets of 5 reps, but I think they came up with something similar at some point. Many coaches attribute the invention of the 5 x 5 system to Bill Starr and his famous book "The Strongest Shall Survive: Strength Training for Football". Here is a quote and the original template from the book:

"These are 3 basic exercises used by weightlifters to increase their strength....the football player (and you can insert Martial Artist, Fighter, whatever there) must work for overall body strength as opposed to specific strengthening exercises....In other words the athlete should be building total leg strength rather than just stronger hamstrings. He should be seeking overall strength in his shoulder girdle rather than just stronger deltoids....the program is fast, simple and, most importantly, effective. It requires very little space and a minimum of equipment...."

Bill Starr's 5X5 Routine in Its Original Form
Monday – Heavy
Power cleans – 5 sets of 5
Bench – 5 sets of 5, then 1×10 with weight from 3rd set (add 10 rep sets after 8-12 weeks on program)
Squats – 5 sets of 5, then 1×10 with weight from 3rd set

(Set 1 - 35% of target / set 2 - 70% of target / set 3 - 80% of target / set 4 - 90% of target / set 5 - target)

Wednesday – Light
Power cleans – 5 sets of 5
Incline Bench – 5 sets of 5, then 1×10 with weight from 3rd set
Squats – 5 sets of 5, then 1×10 with weight from 3rd set
(Set 5 - use weight from 3rd set of Monday)

Friday – Medium
Power cleans – 5 sets of 5
Overhead press – 5 sets of 5, then 1×10 with weight from 3rd set
Squats – 5 sets of 5, then 1×10 with weight from 3rd set
(Set 4 - use weight from 3rd set of Monday / set 5 - use weight 4th set of Monday)"

As you can see, this template is simple and effective. There are 3 days with almost the same exercises (Bench Press "evolves" in Overhead Press throughout the week). The routine implements Heavy-Light-Medium scheme, which is great for intermediate lifters (for beginners, I think, it would be better to use linear progression increasing weight every session). In addition, you should have noticed that the weight gets ramped up every set. I will talk about this later in this article. The exercises are basic compound lifts in Push-Pull-Legs fashion.

Of course, history of 5 x 5 strength training template does not stop with Bill Starr's version. Another example is Reg Park's 5 x 5 variant. It looks like this:

Reg Park's Three Phase 5×5 Program
"Phase One
45-degree back extension 3×10
Back squat 5×5
Bench press 5×5
Deadlift 5×5
Rest 3-5 minutes between the last 3 sets of each exercise.
Train three days per week for three months.

Phase Two for Bodybuilders*
45-degree back extension 3-4×10
Front squat 5×5
Back squat 5×5
Bench press 5×5
Standing barbell shoulder press 5×5
High pull 5×5

Deadlift 5×5
Standing barbell calf raise 5×25
Rest 2 minutes between sets.
Train three days per week for three months.
* After the basic Phase One, Park had a different set of recommended exercises for aspiring Olympic weightlifters. It used a few different sets and reps, and included lunges and power cleans.

Phase Three for Bodybuilders
45-degree back extension 4×10
Front squat 5×5
Back squat 5×5
Standing barbell shoulder press 5×5
Bench press 5×5
Bent-over barbell row 5×5
Deadlift 5×3
Behind-the-neck press or one-arm dumbbell press 5×5
Barbell curl 5×5
Lying triceps extension 5×8
Standing barbell calf raise 5×25
Rest 2 minutes between sets.
Train three days per week for three months."

This program is quite different from Starr's except the first phase. I really do not know whether phase 2 and 3 will work for the average trainee, but they will take serious effort at least to be accomplished. I know they probably will not work for me as I have quite bad recovery. Another important point is the fact that Reg Park did not recommend ramping up the weight. He recommended 2 warm-up sets and 3 work sets with fixed weight.

Starting Strength by Mark Rippetoe

Another reasonable 5 x 5 program is, again, Mark Rippetoe's Starting Strength. I highly encourage you to read his "Starting Strength" [SS] and "Practical Programming for Strength Training" to understand it more deeply. You already know that SS is one of the best programs for beginners. With some tweaking, it becomes one of the best programs for intermediates, too. In my opinion, Rippetoe's variation of 5 x 5 is much more reasonable than both Starr's and Park's. For advanced trainees though (if their goal is bodybuilding), the program volume may be too low, which can be adjusted with assistance "pump" work. There is no point in including the original template here because it was described in the previous article.

My Experience with 5 x 5

I, personally, was first introduced to the 5 x 5 system by Mike Mahler (it was featured in several articles in his e-book "Aggressive Strength Solution for Size and Strength"). It was something really new for me. At that time, I was used only to basic 3 x 10, classic bodybuilding-style and HIT-style work. I was so brainwashed in those days that I thought it was impossible to gain muscle on low repetitions. To my great surprise, 5 x 5 worked and worked very well. That is how I found my love with strength training. From the time I discovered it, I use some variation of 5 x 5 in almost all of my programs. This is what works for me.

5 x 5 Methods Explained

Basically, there are three methods of organizing the 5 x 5 template:
- 4 warm-up sets of 5 working towards 1 top work set of 5;
- 2 warm-up sets of 5 and 3 work sets of 5 with fixed weight;
- Several warm-up sets and 5 sets of 5 with fixed weight.

Every one of them has its own application. 5 sets of 5 with fixed weight requires less intensity because it has more volume, but it may not be suitable for some people. They just might not get all the reps in all the sets no matter what they do. Their sets may look like 5, 5, 5, 5, 3. The second variant is much more suitable for them. The first variant has less volume with working weight, which can be used effectively in light and mid days because you have only one set of practice with working weight.

NOTE: Here is a method of progression I learned from legendary Brooks Kubik. You can start with 4 warm-up sets of 5 and 1 working set. The next session you can do 3 warm-up sets and 2 working sets. Then the next session you can do 2 warm-up sets and 3 working sets. Then add weight and start over with 1 working set of 5. Here is a picture to make it more visual:

Warm-Up	Worksets
4 x 5	1 x 5
3 x 5	2 x 5
2 x 5	3 x 5
Start over	

In addition, despite the examples above, 5 x 5 is not only for full-body routines. You can successfully use it with splits. Iron Addict's SPBR is one of the examples.

5 x 5 and Calisthenics

Regular 5 x 5 routines are great when it comes to weights, but what about calisthenics? Well, everything is a little bit trickier (as always). 5 x 5 will definitely help you build strength in bodyweight movements, but great chances are that you will need to use a more flexible scheme. It is all because you cannot make micro adjustments like with barbell exercises. There are 2 ways out:
1. Weighted calisthenics
2. Use a more flexible set/rep scheme

Both of them were discussed earlier in the book.

Rough Strength Variation of 5 x 5

Of course, I cannot leave you without a routine and practical knowledge on how to use 5 x 5. Here is a way to implement several training tools and several methods of 5 x 5, and a program for intermediate-level trainee for gaining strength and building some muscle:

Day 1
A) Sandbag Zercher Squats 3 x 5
B) Tuck Planche Push-Ups (between chairs) 3 x 5
C) One-Arm Kettlebell Rows 5 x 5
D) Ring Triceps Extensions 3 x 8-12
Day 2 – off

Day 3 – off

Day 4
A1) Kettlebell Double Lunges 5 x 5 (each leg)
A2) Kettlebell Double Swings 5 x 5
B) Pistols 1 x maximum (each leg)
C) One-Leg Calf Raises 3 x 12-20

Day 5
A1) Handstand Push-Ups 3 x 5
A2) Weighted Chin-Ups 3 x 5
B) Weighted Dips 1 x 5
C) Sandbag Shouldering 5 x 2 (1 per side, switch sides after every set)

Day 6 off

Day 7 off

Repeat.

Notes:
- 1 x 5 means 4 warm up sets and 1 work set;
- 3 x 5 means 2-3 warm up sets and 3 work sets;
- 5 x 5 means 2-3 warm up sets and 5 work sets;
- If you cannot accomplish all reps in the work sets in the first week, you are using weights or exercises that are too hard for you;
- If you can accomplish all the reps in work sets, you can add the minimum increment. No more than 2.5 kg;
- If you want to add some muscle, then you need to be in a caloric surplus and eat enough protein and carbs.

Closing Thoughts

This is by no means the last word in 5 x 5 training, but I hope I opened some new ways to train for you, and made the 5 x 5 system more understandable. Use these programs and see what works.

"ONE SKILL A DAY" TRAINING PROGRAM

Have you ever had this feeling that your training is going nowhere? Are you still torturing your body with the same old program you were using for last 5 years of training? Are you sincerely amazed with the lack of results? Ok, enough questions. We both have definitely been in such a situation. You have been doing 3 full-body workouts per week for a really long time. Then they just stop working. You get an epiphany and try some sort of Upper/Lower Split. Your gains skyrocket to the stratosphere and your reason to live seems to have been restored. You think that you have found The Program. However, after a decent amount of time the story repeats itself. You get frustrated, and maybe depressed, one more time. What to do? There are many ways out. I would like to discuss one of them. What if you could train every day (or almost every day), and get outstanding results? Seems too good to be true, but my solution fits the previous sentence perfectly. Enter "One Skill a Day" Training Program.

One Skill a Day?
Yep. In one sentence:
Pick 6 skills you want to improve, and train them 6 days per week, one skill per day.

So, basically, you take 6 skills and spread them throughout the week in such a manner, that you will be concentrating only on one skill per day. In addition, I think that with high-frequency programs it is important to leave one day off. So your week can look like this:

Monday – Skill 1
Tuesday – Skill 2
Wednesday – Skill 3
Thursday – Skill 4

Friday – Skill 5
Saturday – Skill 6
Sunday – Off

How to pick up the skills? We can divide all the human movement patterns very roughly into Upper Body Push, Upper Body Pull and Leg moves. So the number "six" fits magically here, and you can pick 2 Upper Body Pushing exercises, 2 Upper Body Pulling exercises and 2 Leg exercises. Your week now may look like this:

Monday – Upper Body Push 1
Tuesday – Upper Body Pull 1
Wednesday – Legs 1
Thursday – Upper Body Push 2
Friday – Upper Body Pull 2
Saturday – Legs 2
Sunday – Off

There are some modifications you can make but more on this later.

Then you pick up the actual skills you want to improve and put them into appropriate category. Let us assume that you want to improve the Double Kettlebell Snatch, Planche, Sandbag Military Press, Weighted Pistol, One-Arm Chin-Up and Front Lever. In this particular case, your week should look something like this:

Monday – Planche
Tuesday – One-Arm Chin-Up
Wednesday – Double Kettlebell Snatch
Thursday – Sandbag Military Press
Friday – Front Lever
Saturday – Weighted Pistol
Sunday – Off

Of course, I used these exercises just as an example. You need to pick your own and/or scale the intensity.

What is next? Sets and reps. For this particular program, I would recommend flexible set/rep scheme - the one that was described earlier in the book. I feel that it is much more suitable for this program than any set in stone set/rep template. Regarding training volume, I would not go higher than 15-20 total reps in these skills.

Let us get back to our example. Assume that you planned to perform 15 total reps per leg in the Weighted Pistol. As this is strength work, I would start with a weight you can lift for 5-6 reps maximum, and stick with it until

I do all 15. Again, assume that you can perform 6 repetitions with a 32 kg kettlebell. So your session can look like this:

Set 1 – 5 reps (leave one in the tank)
Set 2 – 5 reps
Set 3 – 3 reps
Set 4 – 2 reps
Total: 15 reps

NOTE: *If you are training static holds, then you obviously need a time prescription. I would say that 15-20 reps total roughly equals 30-60 seconds total. Make all the adjustments.*

Is it all? When you feel that you have no energy, you can do just this and call it a day. Most of the time however, I like to add assistance work. By "assistance work" I mean 1-2 exercises that can help you improve the skill you are training. For example, after performing all the sets of Front Lever Holds you can add Front Lever Raises from the full hang and Ice-Cream Makers.

I would do assistance work for 2-3 sets of 8-12 reps. Scale the intensity accordingly.

Let us finish our example program. I will use hypothetical strength levels; you owe me a beer if it is perfect for you:

Monday
A) Advanced Tuck Planche Hold – 30 sec total
B) Tuck Planche Push-Ups – 3 sets of 8

Tuesday
A) One-Arm Chin-Up 90 Degree Holds – 30 sec total
B) Rope Climbs 3 sets of maximum

Wednesday
A) Double Kettlebell Snatches – 12 reps total
B) Double Kettlebell Swings – 3 sets of 12

Thursday
A) Sandbag Military Presses – 15 reps total
B) Kettlebell Alternating Military Presses – 3 sets of 8

Friday
A) One-Leg Front Lever Holds – 30 sec total
B) Advanced Tuck Front Lever Raises – 3 sets of 8

Saturday
A) Weighted Pistols – 15 reps total (per leg)
B) Sandbag Zercher Squats – 3 sets of 8

Sunday
Off

Again, this is just an example. I cannot possibly know what your strength levels are, so you need to do some homework.

How Did I Come Up with This?

It is nothing new. Such programs existed a long time before I was born. Like we say here in Ukraine: "Everything new is well-forgotten old". Sometimes you need to be reminded about something to understand its value.

Lots of athletes used some sort of high-frequency training with success for decades. Arnold and Sergio Oliva, the all-mighty Bulgarians, Pyotr Kryloff and Arthur Saxon, Eugene Sandow, and plenty of others. The important thing was to make it work for average genetics, which I think I accomplished by restricting volume.

Why So Often?

High-frequency programs always work awesome for me, and for my clients. The problem usually is with time. I know that it is lame excuse. However, sometimes you just cannot commit to training every day because of some reasons that are out of your control. Anyway, if you are used to training 3 times per week and hit a plateau, then high-frequency training can be your lucky way out. In my experience, high-frequency training is a good way to gain more strength through neural adaptation, build more muscle through increased training volume and lean out a bit through burning more calories (more often).

Why Only One Skill?

Because given the intensity is high, this will be enough. Maybe you will be able to do more than one skill in future, but I really doubt it. If intensity and frequency are high, then volume should be low. It is law.

What Modification Can You Make?

You can mix and match quantities of movement patterns, but use no more than 3 per type. For example, when you are unable to perform leg work, you can pick 3 Upper Body Pushes, 3 Upper Body Pulls, and just alternate them. You get the idea.

Despite this modification, I insist that you should use the program as laid out earlier in this article. I understand that this can be impossible for certain category of people due to some disability or a different reason, but I do not want this modification information be a way to escape leg work (or some other type of work you don't enjoy, but should be doing).

How to Go Absolutely Nuts with It?

You can use the modification above and take it further. Just a quick warning: use this information only if you are completely sure that you will have a steady income of food, lots of sleep, and minimum stress in the following weeks. Otherwise, stick to the original plan.

Ok, so to go absolutely nuts we will need a twice-a-day approach. We will pick 3 Upper Body Push exercises, 3 Upper Body Pulls, and 3 Leg exercises. We can program it this way:

Monday
AM - *Upper Body Push 1*
PM - *Legs 1*

Tuesday
Upper Body Pull 1

Wednesday
AM - *Legs 2*
PM - *Upper Body Push 2*

Thursday
Upper Body Pull 2

Friday
AM - *Upper Body Push 3*
PM - *Legs 3*

Saturday
Upper Body Pull 3

Sunday - *Off*

It should be around 4-6 hours between AM and PM workouts. If possible, take a nap. And don't forget to eat enough calories and protein.

My Actual Program

To show you that this program is not some piece of junk, I will share the actual routine I was following at the moment of writing this article. It was created using the principles I laid out above. Here it is:

Day 1
AM
A) One-Arm Chin-Up Progression (I varied exercises every week)
B) Rope Climbing
C) Back Lever Pull-Outs on Dip Bars (optional)
PM
A) Double Kettlebell Swings

Day 2
A) Free-Standing Handstand Push-Ups Progression
B) 2 Finger Sliding POAPU
C) Kettlebell Alternating Military Presses (or some other kettlebell press; optional)

Day 3
AM
A) Front Lever Holds
B) Front Lever Raises
C) Ice-Cream Makers (optional)
PM
A) Double Kettlebell Squats

Day 4
A) 5 Finger Assisted OAHSPU
B) Double Kettlebell Military Press (or Push Press, or Jerk)
C) Claw Fingertip Push-Ups

Day 5
AM
A) Controlled Bar Muscle-Ups
B) False Grip Pull-Ups
C) Russian Dips
PM
A) One-Arm Kettlebell Snatches

Day 6
A) Planches
B) Straddle Planche Push-Ups
C) Triceps Extensions

Some days when I felt absolutely no energy, I did just the skill and screwed everything else. However, most of the time my current training looked exactly like this.

Closing Thoughts

So there you have it. If you struggle with your training or everything pisses you off, the "One Skill a Day" Program can be the perfect solution. You should not use this program if you do not have at least 40 minutes to train 6 days per week because everybody has different conditions. If you do have it, then crush it and acquire the gains you deserved.

NUTRITION

HIGH-PROTEIN DIET ON A BUDGET

If you are a hard training athlete or just an ordinary fitness enthusiast that is trying to gain strength, build muscle and lose fat, high-protein diet would probably be the best option for you (of course, if you have no kidney diseases). However, have you ever wondered how the hell you are supposed to follow high-protein diet and do not spend all your income on it? How to make it happen? I will try to answer these questions here and show you how I made a high-protein diet more affordable for me here in Ukraine.

What Is a High-Protein Diet?

Any diet that consists of at least 1 g of protein per 1 lb (2.2 kg) of bodyweight is considered high in protein. Some people will argue, but let us stick with this definition. To create a high-protein diet we will need a minimum of two stats: bodyweight and maintenance calories. Of course, the more info we take into account, the better diet plan we can create, but these two will give us a start.

So let's use me as example. At the moment of writing this article my stats were:

Weight: 82.5 kg (181.5 lb)

Maintenance: ~2500 kcal per day

As you can see, the bare minimum of protein per day for this example is approximately 180 grams (approx. 1 g per 1 lb). If I want to gain muscle, I will need to increase it to approximately 270 grams, and maybe even more (well, you may need less on several occasions, but I will discuss this later). If I want to lose some fat, I am ok with 180 grams.

How to Create Your Own High-Protein Diet?

So the next step would be to create a menu that will satisfy our protein requirements. First of all, you should choose your protein sources. They could be either animal, or plant based. In my experience, animal protein products are far superior to plants. I am not sure whether it is because of the incompleteness of plant protein sources or any other reason, but I see fewer results in muscle building and fat burning when eating plants compared to tasty dead animals and their products.

Additionally, if you think that plant-based diet is cheaper, here is some simple math for you. The other day I had a conversation with a guy who wanted to try vegetarian (and possibly vegan) diet. We sat down and counted *value of 1 gram of protein [V1gP]* for different food sources. The lower the value – the cheaper the protein source. Why did I use value of 1 gram of protein? Obviously, because protein is the most useful nutrient as well as the most expensive. Here are the rough numbers from several foods. I used FitDay.com as the calorie counter:

- *Chicken breast (complete protein source)*: 1 kg costs ~40 UAH (~$5). It contains ~315 g of protein (fried). $V1gP$ = ***0.13** UAH*;
- *Turkey breast (complete protein source)*: 1 kg costs ~60 UAH (~$7.5). It contains also ~315 g of protein (fried). $V1gP$ = ***0.19** UAH*;
- *Pork (complete protein source)*: 1 kg costs ~60 UAH (~$7.5). It contains 265 g of protein (fried). $V1gP$ = ***0.23** UAH*;
- *Beef (complete protein source)*: 1 kg costs ~65 UAH (~$8). It contains 300 g of protein (fried). $V1gP$ = ***0.22** UAH*;
- *Salmon (complete protein source)*: 1 kg costs ~100 UAH (~$12.5). It contains 185 g of protein (fried). $V1gP$ = ***0.54** UAH*;
- *Almonds (incomplete protein source)*: 1 kg costs ~130 UAH (~$12.5). It contains 210 g of protein (raw). $V1gP$ = ***0.62** UAH*;
- *Eggs (complete protein source)*: 10 eggs cost ~10 UAH (~$1). It contains 62 g of protein (fried). $V1gP$ = ***0.16** UAH*;
- *Split Peas (incomplete protein source)*: 1 kg costs ~4 UAH (~$0.5). It contains 245 g of protein (raw). $V1gP$ = ***0.02** UAH*.

As you can see, chicken breast is the cheapest option. "But what about split peas?" – you may ask. They have an incomplete amino acid profile, twice as many carbohydrates as protein, and they taste like crap. Therefore, claims that vegetarian/vegan diet is cheaper are lies.

As experience shows, the top protein-food sources are:
- Meat
- Poultry
- Fish
- Eggs
- Cottage cheese

I like to keep it simple and not add any fancy stuff. Regarding actual products, the cheapest picks are:
- chicken breast;
- 0% cottage cheese (although it tastes like shit (I'm not saying that I've

tasted shit, but I guess that it may taste even better than this devil's trick));
- 9.5% cottage cheese;
- 17% cottage cheese (it tastes awesome);
- eggs.

I can also add here lean beef, lean pork, and fish, but they cost more for their macronutrient profile. Additionally, I would not eat canned food, and we do not have the organic craze here. So I do not really know whether my food is organic or not. As the proverb says: "The less you know - the better you sleep".

The next step would be to create menus for workout and non-workout days according to calories and protein needs. I like to add some carbs on workout days and to go low-carb on non-workout days. Workout days should have generally more calories, and non-workout - less. The fastest way to create a menu is to use a calorie counter like, again, FitDay.com. All you need to do is to take the foods you eat on a daily basis and combine proper amounts of them to get the desired calories and protein.

For example, here are two menus for fat loss for me or someone with my stats:

1) WO Day
250 g fried chicken breast
230 g 9.5% cottage cheese
6 fried eggs
250 g 17% cottage cheese with dry fruits
130 g rice (I measure it dry before boiling; it's half a cup)
+ any amount of veggies
Total: 2549 kcal
Protein: 187 g
Cost: 40 UAH ($5) per day

2) Non-WO Day
10 hard-boiled eggs (you may think "holy shit!", but I just love eggs and their price)
460 g 0% cottage cheese
250 g 17% cottage cheese with dry fruits
+ any amount of veggies
Total: 2013 kcal
Protein: 186 g
Cost: 40 UAH ($5) per day

As you can see, such a diet will cost me $150 per month. There are not any supplements included, and there is a reason for that. When we are talking about dieting on a budget, food should be your number one priority.

In addition, you should think about variety; once you hit a plateau, you will need to create new menus.

Intermittent Fasting and High-Protein Diet

I am a big proponent of intermittent fasting. It keeps you energized, it promotes fat loss, it trains your mind and your body, it gives you freedom, it keeps you full and satisfied and it regulates your hormones to name just a few advantages. Another great thing about it is that while you are fasting and not eating protein, your sensitivity to it increases. According to Ori Hofmekler, author of the Warrior Diet, protein absorption during periods of overfeeding preceded by underfeeding periods increases up to 160%. That is quite big advantage for me. However, as with everything in life, intermittent fasting is not for everyone. I would not recommend it for people with fast metabolism and weak-minded losers.

Closing Thoughts

So now you have all the keys to create your own high-protein diet and no excuses. A high-protein diet should not be expensive as many may think. Make smart food choices and spend all the saved money on strippers and booze.

6 BIGGEST DIET FLAWS

There are more "diet-conscious" people than ever nowadays. The funny thing is that there are also more fat people than ever. There are several reasons for that, but the thing I would like to address is that people concentrate on the small picture while ignoring the big one. What if I tell you that all those "diet" or "low-fat" foods and drinks are not the answer to your fat loss? In many cases, they just slow down your progress. I often get questions like these:

"Is rye bread better than wheat?"
"What if I add freshly-squeezed lemon juice to my meal?"
"How many pieces of grapefruit should I eat per day for optimal fat loss?"

Stop it. You are just wasting your time and mine. None of this stuff matters. It just pisses me off. Minor tweaks work only if the big picture is in check. So in this article, I would like to share with you my version of what are the biggest diet flaws.

Sugar

I guess this is one of the biggest flaws in any diet. Sugar is bad. Of course, if you have great genetics and you are already ripped and muscular, then feel free to eat it as much as you want. Your health will not be very happy though. Diabetes is just one of many problems caused by excessive sugar consumption. You can argue: "Hey! I can eat it in moderation" Well, yes, you can. However, as experience shows, you will not be able to reach maximum leanness with sugar if you have crappy genetics (as I do). So get rid of it and forget it. You do not need it if you want to get lean and stay in shape. If you want to get or remain fat, feel free to eat as much sugar as you want. The same thing goes for fructose, juices, and sugar drinks. Fuck'em!

Ultra-Low Calorie Diet

Many people wake up one day, look at themselves in the mirror, and think: "How the fuck could this happen to me? I look like a pile of fucking fat!" That's the time when most of them decide to eat nothing (or almost nothing). Bad idea. Most of them do not realize yet that by eating nothing for long periods of time, they slow down their metabolism (according to Lyle McDonald, metabolism slows down after 3-4 days of ultralow-calorie dieting). Sounds like nothing scary. In reality it is. These people drop some fat, but also with substantial amounts of muscle loss. Say, 5 kg total. Rarely can they take much longer than several weeks. What happens next? They come back to their shitty eating habits and gain back those 5 kg, but almost exclusively fat. In addition to that, they gain 4-5 kg of fat more, because their metabolism has slowed down. *Take-home point: stay away from ultra-low calorie diets.*

Highly Processed Foods

It seems like everybody loves highly processed foods. They are tasty and they smell good. However, you can eat like a ton of them and be hungry in an hour. They do not satiate you at all, and are not absorbed well by your body. That is why so many fat people are regular fast-food eaters. Nature intended that we should be eating raw food. I am not saying here that we should eat only raw meat or raw eggs, no. However, our food should be minimally processed.

Wrong Amount of Calories

The basic law of thermodynamics works. Calories in vs calories out. If we burn more calories than we consume, then we would be losing weight. If we burn less than we consume, then we would be gaining weight. It is not always that simple, but basically it is always like that. Consume the wrong amount of calories for your goal and you will fail. If your goal is to gain muscle, then add 10-20% to your maintenance amount of calories per day. If your goal is to lose fat, then subtract 10-20% from your maintenance amount of calories per day. Decide from there.

Wrong Macronutrients

Proteins, Carbs and Fats. With high amount of available information on this theme, you can easily screw up in your macronutrient ratios. Some say that carbs are evil; others say that fat is bad and some of them even say that protein isn't good. Opinions like assholes, remember? So let me show you another one.

As my experience shows, protein is the best macronutrient of all. I received a chance to lean out only with high to ultra-high doses of protein, which was 270-300 g per day for me. You should note that I am not selling you anything here. These numbers were acquired purely from food, no supplements. Moreover, most of knowledgeable coaches use such doses as requirement for muscle growth.

As for carbs, they are not that evil as low-carb gurus tell you. Of course, you will need an intelligent carb cycling plan if you want to be lean, but you don't need to fear carbs like death itself.

As for fats, you need them for your hormones to work properly.

One more thing: carbs and fats are both sources of energy that are absorbed by different enzymes (according to Ori Hofmekler). It is probably not the best idea to mix high quantities of fats and carbs. You will just confuse your body. However, it is a minor tweak (for some people this tweak is not so minor, but for the overweight majority there is nothing to worry about fats and carbs together while protein is high).

Relying on Supplements

I hear this very often: "I'll buy some protein powder to gain some muscle". What if I told you that you don't need protein powders to build muscle? It will be just a waste of money if your training and diet are bad. Supplements were created to *supplement* your training and diet, not to replace them. Use them only for convenience. I would rather go with food than with supplements (more on this in the next article).

Closing Thoughts

So now you get it. Again, flush all your sugar in the toilet, avoid ultra-low calorie diets like the plague, forget about highly-processed foods, use the right amount of calories for your goal, use the right macronutrient ratios, and stop relying on supplements. This way you will get to your goal in the fastest manner possible and will be healthy along the way.

SUPPLEMENTS. DO YOU REALLY NEED THEM?

The buzz about supplements nowadays is hilarious, in my opinion. You can read about them everywhere.

"Gain 20 pounds of lean muscle with our brand new protein!"

"Scientifically approved supplement will scorch your fat away in 4 weeks! Especially in the belly region!"

"Only our NO-booster will give that skin-tearing pump, your arms will grow bigger and 900% faster!"

How many times have you heard that? Some claims are pretty ridiculous. However, people believe those claims again and again, meanwhile supporting supplement manufacturers. It is business after all.

What is the Problem with Supplements?

There is only one problem with them. People have a tendency to overcomplicate things and to give them more value than they can really provide. Supplements are really what they are. They just SUPPLEMENT your training, diet and restoration. You can take all the supplements in the world and get zero results. You need to know where, when, and how to use them. Do not expect miracle gains if you take powdered protein. Do not expect miracle fat loss if you take some "scientifically proven" fat-burner. Attaining a better body is hard work. If you do not plan to inject tons of illegal performance-enhancing substances, then prepare for war.

Focus on the Big Three: Training, Diet and Recovery. I am a big believer that you actually need NO supplements to gain strength, build muscle and get ripped. In other words, you can make it rough. There are so many people that follow all the new supplements on the market while forget to devote adequate time for their training, nutrition and recovery. Supplements are luxury. The sooner you understand this, the faster you start getting results.

I actually was there. A long time ago, I was also obsessed with all that supplement-buzz. All the bodybuilding magazines preach that crap. You need protein powder. You need amino acids. You need transport systems. You need creatine. All that stuff. What a joke! Look at all the mighty men of the past. People were athletic and muscular without supplements. So why do you need them after all?

When Do You Really Need Supplements?

The important point here is that I did not say that supplements are evil and you should avoid them like the plague. I am saying that people are too obsessed with them. There are times when you *can* use supplements. However, you should fit one or several conditions below:

1. You have extra cash.

You can start using supplements only (I mean ONLY) when you have extra money, and you do not have any idea what to spend it on. If you are short on money, forget about them and focus on real healthy food in the first place. It works like this: if you have money, you need to buy food, spend it on your girlfriend/family, and have some fun. Only after that should you consider purchasing supplements.

2. You have some health problems that can be overcome with supplements.

There are situations in life when people need supplementation for medical purposes.

3. You understand that supplements will not bring you superhuman results.

It is simple. Training, Diet and Recovery first, supplements next. They can enhance performance a bit, but expect nothing extraordinary. It is a sure way to frustration.

So now you really want to use supplementation. What to choose?

Rough Strength's number one choice will be *fish oil*. The benefits of this supplement are big. Your health, hormones, cardiovascular system, and mood will improve. No need to waste time and space on counting the benefits of fish oil. If you have the money and desire, this one should be your number one priority.

You should take about 6-12 g per day of quality fish oil. Recent studies [16] show increase in muscle protein synthesis if you take about 2 g EPA/1.5 g DHA per day. So choose your supplements wisely. Read the label. Also, I consider it not a bad idea to take 1 tbsp of flaxseed oil per day too.

Vitamin C should be next in the queue. It is an anti-oxidant, and it helps with fighting diseases. It is required in multiple essential metabolic reactions in your body and more.

You can take several grams of high quality vitamin C per day. Yet no more than 500 mg of a crappy one. Well, you can also use a high quality multivitamin supplement as well.

Digestive enzymes would be my next choice. They help with digestion, cure GI tract problems, and fight inflammation all over the body. It is definitely wise supplement choice.

After that, if you have money and desire left, you can experiment with other supplements, but take care of your health first. The healthier you are the more gains you can expect. Remember: no supplements can substitute training, diet and restoration.

You can also use protein supplements for convenience. No need to get too fancy though. My choice would be casein with at least 80% protein. That should do. There are other effective protein supplements, but they are too expensive for their value in my opinion.

The Perfect Supplement Mix

Not long time ago, I found the perfect supplement mix for me, which works every time I use it. *It is multivitamin + fish oil*. The last time, I used Universal Nutrition Animal Pak and some Ukrainian brand of liquid fish oil (there is only one here). Dosing protocol was 1 bag of Animal Pak with first meal (never taken on an empty stomach; I get a severe headache from this) and 2 tablespoons of fish oil before bed or with your last meal.

What are the effects? Hard wood every morning (if you know what I mean), elevated mood that feels something near to happiness, increased energy, and feeling that your hormones are in tune (if you possibly can get such feeling). However, you should understand that in my case, this supplement mix was added to intermittent fasting, proper calories and macronutrient ratios, as well as a sound training program. It may not work for you if you failed one of those.

Also, I should warn you that the *effect is gradual*. I began to feel any effect after a week or so of supplementation.

Who will benefit from this mix? Let me share you my story. The first time I seriously experimented with a multivitamin/fish oil mix was during the spring/summer of 2012. I felt like a million bucks. My testosterone was pretty high, I guess. My sex drive and energy were through the roof. My mood was always good. You know, it is that feeling when you want to create, when you feel unstoppable, when you want to make jokes, and anytime you see hot chick you have hardness in your pants. Then due to an increase of work at my demanding daily job, I dropped the experimentation. All the effects also went down.

In April of 2013, I was at a really dark place. I had no energy, I was always angry; I almost had no sex drive. Something had to change. So I dropped that shitty job and never looked back. The day I did it, I instantly felt better, but nothing close to the feeling I described above. Then unexpectedly I got back to the multivitamin/fish oil mix and that was the perfect time to feel the difference. I was really hooked. It worked like a charm. All the effects were back.

So I would recommend this supplementation for the people that have demanding jobs and low energy and sex drive. Try it and let me know how it worked for you.

MENTAL ASPECTS

YOUR WORST ENEMY

So you've been training for some time. You have made some gains. In strength, in muscle, in fat loss. However, after few weeks you stopped progressing. No amount of bench pressing, curls and crunches can make you move forward again. You blame everyone for your failures. You blame bad genetics, a crappy gym environment, the wrong lunar phase, government, etc. However, the reality is quite opposite. You just suck, and suck hard. And your program sucks. And, of course, your diet sucks too. As well as your overall approach to everything in life.

Guess Who Is Your Worst Enemy?

You and only you. Never blame anyone except yourself for your failures. You are the only person who can take action over your life (or take no action at all), and that is the person you should blame. There is a good proverb: "If you want to change something, start with yourself". So start.

I am a big believer in hard work. If you want to get something valuable out of any endeavor, then you should put some serious work into it. As my experience shows, this rule can be applied to any situation in life. If you can get something without any effort, then you will not understand its value. There are tons of people with better than average genetics, but they do not appreciate what they have because they did not pay the price of hard work. Additionally, ask any successful entrepreneur about hard work, and he will explain you what it is.

And if you think that you do not need to put in hard work to get results, think again. I had a conversation with one clearly fat woman about diet some time ago. After my tips on the right diet approach, the person who I was consulting said to me: "You know, holidays are coming, and I won't be doing all the stuff you told me". So I replied: "No big deal. You'll just remain fat and ugly". I do not care whether it is a holiday or not. Holidays are 2-3 days out of each month at most. You have at least 26 days to eat right, so do not fool yourself or anybody else. You are fat because of you. You are weak because of you. You have no muscle also because of you.

The Importance of Understanding

Processes in your body do not get any better with time and never will. Your metabolism gets worse and worse every day. You will get fatter and fatter with age, unless you are a lucky ripped bastard. You need to understand that if you are not happy with your health/strength/look, then you are doing something wrong. You need to cultivate the habit of exercising and eating right. And yes, you will need to exercise and eat healthy until you die. There is no way around this. If you think that you will just do everything right for 3 months or so, and then get back to your old sitting-and-eat-all-the-cakes routine, then you are totally wrong. There is no quick fix. Bring back the bad habit, and you will get back to where you started in no time. It may sound rough, but the truth is what is important.

WHY DO PEOPLE FAIL TO GET RESULTS?

Why do people fail to get results? Well, there could be several reasons for that. The most common are lack of a plan and a lack of discipline. My intention here is to help you not make those mistakes.

Lack of a Plan

Ask any serious entrepreneur to help you start a new business, and he'll most likely ask you for a business-plan. Why? If you have no plan, then you have no predictable results. The same goes for training and nutrition. Yes, there are several other factors (like genetics that give you the unique opportunity to perform bullshit at your training sessions, eat total crap, and still grow and lose fat), but no plan still transfers to a lack of results. Well, you do not need to be TOO precise. Be prepared that some workouts will go wrong, some workouts will differ from your plan, and some days you will not have a chance not to eat crap. Nevertheless, the general strategy should remain stable.

Believe it or not, a training log is the best thing you can do for your training, as well as keeping a food log is the best thing you can do to your nutrition. If you really want results, you need the right program and nutrition plan that suits your individual needs, goals, and restrictions. You may train spontaneously and get results, but it is really a matter of luck. What will you rely more on: luck or a plan? Well, I think that the answer is obvious.

Take-home point: if you have been training for some time and still get no measurable results, maybe it is time to invest in a training and food log. Get a plan!

Lack of Discipline

This is big. Even huge. This is everywhere: motivational pictures and motivational videos. Give me a break! While there are some videos that really motivate you to act, most of them are useless. You just need discipline to do something right. *If you want to be strong and/or look awesome, you will need to follow some rules until the end of your days. Deal with it!* Terrified? Well, then you are weak and you will remain weak forever. Discipline is strength. I am sick and tired of people that want to get strong and muscular but do not have the discipline to train hard and especially eat right amounts of food and protein. I am sick and tired of people that want to lose fat and do not have the discipline to stick to simple diet plan. Train for strength. Eat a bit less if you want to lose fat; eat a bit more if you want to build muscle; eat high-protein, repeat. Does it really sound so difficult?

Closing Thoughts

Take a look around. Weak people are surrounding you everywhere. They all look for a magic pill to solve their problems. The truth is that there is no such pill. Do not be one of them. Be strong. Have a plan of attack. Have the discipline to follow your plan until you die. Then you will be strong and muscular forever. It is that simple.

WARRIOR ATTITUDE TO TRAINING AND NUTRITION

I am sick and tired of what I see. I do not know what situation is in your country/city, but chances are that you see the same picture. I will tell you what I see here in Ukraine. Almost everyone drinks alcohol in excessive amounts and/or daily. It is not far from the truth if I say that every 1 out of 3 people here are alcoholics. I have nothing against drinking in moderation, but when people crap in their pants because they are so drunk, it is not right. Almost everyone smokes cigarettes daily. Lots of people smoke weed. Many people drink energy-drinks daily. This is considered normal here. I see weak fat people everywhere. Everyone who tells you otherwise about this country is fucking hypocrite.

Usually, when people get a reality check and realize that they are weak fat maggots, they decide to start 'healthy' eating. They believe all the dieting hype: they do not eat after 6PM, they do not eat fried food, they do not eat fats or carbs, etc. Yet at the same time, they still drink alcohol, energy drinks, chain smoke, and sleep for 3-4 hours per day, because all their time is devoted to surfing social networks. Of course, this approach does not work and they decide to go to gym. At first, these people are full of motivation. They think that if they destroy themselves in the gym for 2-3 hours per day, which in reality is low-intensity machine shit and endless treadmill crap, they will get 'in shape' in several weeks. Of course, they get another reality check.

Most of them create excuses for themselves at this point. They say: "I've tried it all. It doesn't work for me!" after couple of weeks. Smarter ones understand that they are wasting their time. They start looking for personal training services. This is the first right decision. However, here comes another problem: not every personal trainer is good. An intelligent trainer that knows what he is doing, 'practices what he preaches', and educates himself daily is one in a million. And this is not all. Even when these weak fat people get to such trainer, chances are that they will not get results because they lack discipline and are lazy bastards. They think if they got brilliant trainer, then results will follow by themselves. *You need to put in HARD WORK if you want results!* It seems like no one understands this nowadays. That is why I see women that are stronger than men. People that sell themselves for ultra-convenience that they do not need. Ignorance, stupidity, immaturity and idleness are what I see.

Get a Warrior Attitude

What I mean by warrior attitude? I mean not being a weak fat pussy. Take charge of your life. Remember, you (and only you, not anybody else) are the one who is responsible for your current strength, look, and life. You probably do not possess the worst genetics in the world and you are not doomed to be fat and weak. *Get a warrior attitude to life, training, and nutrition!*

Don't like your job? Quit. Find something you like to do.

Don't like your relationship? Make it better. Can't? Don't waste another person's life.

Want to look awesome? Get to the gym.

Don't have time or money for the gym? Fuck that, get your own! Buy a pair of kettlebells. Expensive? Make a sandbag. I got my recent sandbag for under $5.

Don't have sand? Fill it with something else. Fill it with rice, peas whatever.

Don't have time to make it? Train with your bodyweight.

Don't know how? Get help from an expert. Don't have money? Read RoughStrength.com, educate yourself, read books.

Will you get results just from training? Yes.

Want more? Get a diet. You can get pretty cheap decent diet with some planning and calculating.

"But I can't sleep 8+ hours a day?" Make time.

Still don't have? Fuck it. Go with it. I've seen people get results on 5 hours of sleep per day. And I mean increase in strength, muscle and fat loss. Of course, results will come at much slower pace, but if you make everything right, you'll get them. This is what matters. Be a man. Don't be afraid to make decisions and go against the grain.

Why Do I Like Calisthenics?

It is because they cultivate this warrior attitude in you unintentionally. I will describe what I mean. When I train my bodyweight exercises, it is like battle with myself. Everything around does not matter anymore. Everything that matters at this time is my mind, my body, and resistance. The place where I train becomes my sacred cave. It is the place where I get stronger. The beauty of bodyweight strength training is in fact that this place can be anywhere. Every time I get one more rep or one more set - it is a victory. Every time I do not get stronger, it just makes me hungrier to obtain this strength. With every little victory, I get more mental strength and stability, more understanding of my body, and more control over my life.

With calisthenics, it is actually a little bit harder to visualize resistance. With weights, everything is simple. Here are 180 kg. You need to pick them up from the floor. With bodyweight, everything is a little trickier, but once you get an understanding of how your body moves through space, you get something more than just the ability to lift heavy weights. Calisthenics give you freedom in training and movement. However, do not be afraid to mix them with weights.

Why Do I Like Intermittent Fasting?

Again, because of warrior attitude cultivation. You need warrior discipline to go without eating. You need warrior discipline to deal with hunger. You need warrior discipline to say no to everyone who tries to break your fast without your desire. Intermittent fasting gives you freedom from constant worrying about food and meals. Yes, you will still need to make your diet work but with intermittent fasting, it will be a lot easier. You can eat like a king even on a calorie-restricted diet. Intermittent fasting gives you the mental strength to move through obstacles.

Closing Thoughts

We live in tough times. We can have all the information we want through the internet, but we are too lazy to read. We can fly to another continent in less than 24 hours, but we are too lazy to take stairs instead of elevator. We can gain strength and get the body we want, but we are too lazy to start. Do not be among such a pitiful majority. Be a warrior; take whatever from life that you deserve and nothing less.

STRENGTH TRAINING IN REAL LIFE CIRCUMSTANCES

"...But how should I train when I have so many responsibilities and problems in my life?"

A lot of people requested the answer to this question, so I would like to address it in this article. There is no hard rule on what you should do when you are in such situation, but I'll try to sum up everything that I know on the theme. Anyway, first of all, let us talk about what is "hard"?

What Circumstances Are Considered Hard?

Well, let's face it; almost everybody considers his/her circumstances the hardest possible. Maybe the hardest in the history of mankind. Maybe somebody even uses word combinations like "ultimate hardness" (have you noticed how the word "ultimate" leaves no other chance?). And while this unquestionably means good things if we are talking about the male sex function, this is not appropriate for life conditions. You should understand that everybody has problems. Everybody has responsibilities. And, importantly, you cannot use your circumstances as an excuse not to train or not to eat right.

Watch this video – [17]. If your circumstances are not like these, I do not consider them hard. Have you ever donated blood to train one more time? If not, then shut up and train. There are literally millions of people around the world that have kids, several jobs, barely make money for food and to pay their bills, and still they train hard and eat properly. No matter what. They just do not have any other option. I admire such people.

Here is an example: I met a bodybuilder some time ago. We had a conversation about his career. He told me the story of how he was able to win the bronze prize at the Ukrainian Bodybuilding Championship. Of course, he used unreal doses of steroids at that time, but he had no other choice. Ask any competitive bodybuilder, if you want to compete with the best, you must inject "pharma" because they do. Steroids aside, what he told me is that he was working on two jobs and trained 6 days a week. Sometimes twice per day. He spent lots of money, he was completely sleep-deprived and he barely made the money to sustain this regimen. Anyway, he succeeded and placed third. Was it worth the effort? I don't know. He said that he could easily buy a good car for the money spent on steroids and food (and buying a car is a big deal here in Ukraine). Nevertheless, the main point here is that dedication of this man was unbreakable despite the circumstances, and this deserves respect.

Another example is more real. It is one of my clients. He lives here in Ukraine. He has a kid. He has a family. He has responsibilities. He must pay for rent to keep his family warm. He must pay for food to keep his family full. He must work really hard to make it all happen. Yet still he trains 3 times per week. He has no excuses.

By the way, I did not use their names for personal reasons. I have many other examples of different people who made it despite the hard circumstances. They are ranging from celebrities to ordinary every day heroes. What unites them? They all made training a central part of their lives, and made it work. So how can you also succeed?

Practical Ways to Manage Training and Diet in Real Life

If you are in such a situation, you need to address this question as soon as possible. Otherwise, you will not be able to achieve any reasonable results, which is the most effective demotivator known to me. People always give up on things they do not see measurable results in. And sooner rather than later.

What can you do? First of all, get real. You should understand that you cannot attain results at the same speed as if you did nothing except training, eating and sleeping. Deal with it.

Regarding training. What can you do to make it work?

- If you are training and not getting stronger on a regular basis, then my first choice would be *volume*. Cut it. Leave just 2/3 of sets. Use the Pareto Principle. Leave just 20% of exercises that give you 80% of results. You know what they are. Some kind of press, some kind of row and some kind of squat are all that you need to progress. For example, Military Press, Pull-Up and Sandbag Zercher Squat, and you are good to go.

- If you are still struggling, refer to the Keep-It-Simple Principle. If your training (at any period) gets too sophisticated, you should most definitely review it and make it simpler. It always works.

- If you are still not making progress, the next choice will be *training frequency*. If you are training 3 times per week, already cut the volume and get nothing in terms of results, then it is time to try training 2 times per week or every third day. Feel free to cut the frequency to once every 5 days. From my experience anything less will not work.

- I do not recommend cutting intensity. You should be able to progress managing volume and frequency. If your life gets REALLY hard, you can temporarily decrease intensity. But sometimes it's better to take some rest.

Let us use this information on routine of some hypothetical Rough Strength disciple [HRSD]. Let us assume that his routine is reasonable. Let it be Upper-Lower-Upper split. For example:

Monday
A1) Double Kettlebell Floor Press 3 x 5
A2) Weighted Pull-Up 3 x 5
B1) Weighted Push-Ups 4 x 8
B2) Advanced Tuck Front Lever Rows 4 x 8

Wednesday
A) Sandbag Shoulder Squat 3 x 5 (per side)
B) Double Kettlebell Swings 3 x 6
C1) Ring Triceps Extensions 3 x 12
C2) One-Leg Strict Calf Raises 3 x 12
C3) Towel Curls 3 x 12 (per arm)

Friday
A1) Wall-Assisted Handstand Push-Ups 3 x 6
A2) One-Arm Kettlebell Bent-Over Row 3 x 6
B1) Sandbag Push Press 4 x 8
B2) One-Arm Kettlebell High Pull 3 x 6 (per arm)

And suddenly our HRSD gets twins, gets fired and gets two new jobs to keep his family safe. In such situation, I would cut down the "volume work" first. So now his routine would look like this:

Monday
A1) Double Kettlebell Floor Press 3 x 5
A2) Weighted Pull-Up 3 x 5

Wednesday
A) Sandbag Shoulder Squat 3 x 5 (per side)
B) Double Kettlebell Swings 3 x 6

Friday
A1) Wall-Assisted Handstand Push-Ups 3 x 6
A2) One-Arm Kettlebell Bent-Over Row 3 x 6

Let us assume that he still makes no progress. My next move would be cutting the frequency. For example, Day 1 would be Monday, Day 2 – Thursday instead of Wednesday, Day 3 – Sunday instead of Friday.

If he still makes no progress, I will cut one more set from each exercise. If we have a problem anyway, I will suggest him some rest.

Regarding nutrition. Well, nutrition is very debatable thing. Some people say you need to count calories, some say you do not. Some people say you need to eat high amounts of protein, some say you do not. Some people say that carbs are evil, some say they are not. Your head can explode just from ordinary information search on nutrition. And if you have hard time, you can jump off the cliff just from one thought about it.

So how can you make it easier? There are actually several ways:

- *Do not count calories, make a plan.* It is a pain in the ass to count calories every single fucking day. So instead, I suggest you to make 2-3 daily diet plans and just follow them. It requires nothing but some food weighing and discipline.

- *Go to the food store only 2-3 times per week.* This will save time.

- *If you have average to slow metabolism, follow an intermittent fasting protocol.* This not only will make you leaner, but will save lots of time. You will be cooking only once per day, and you will be eating like a king.

- *Focus on protein.* Sometimes you just cannot get it all right. Focus on protein, because it is the most important macronutrient. Good old meat, eggs, fish and cottage cheese. You will be leaner and bigger.

Again, if something does not work in your nutrition plan, use your analytic skills. If you are too fat, increase your protein intake and cut calories. If you are struggling to gain muscle, then add calories and, again, increase protein intake. Be smart, but don't sweat it.

Coping with Mental Aspects

Hard circumstances are hard not only physically but also mentally. You probably know this. Sometimes you feel that the world is falling apart. Sometimes you feel that you are on the bottom of life. Sometimes you think that it would have been much easier if you had never existed. It is unbearable sometimes. You feel that there will never be any stability in your life. What can I say? I had dark times. Well, I still have them from time to time. What I learnt, is that you need to embrace instability in your life. It is the only way to remain sane. It is easier said than done. However, when you accept the circumstances, stop whining and concentrate on the right things, every piece of the puzzle gets into its own place. *Learn to embrace instability as soon as possible or you will never find inner peace in this world.* It is something that sounds like Buddha, but it is true. You are always free in your mind.

Another thing I would like to mention on mental aspects is the power of exercise. I mean strength training. Strength is all about nervous system, right? That is why, in my opinion, the stronger the person - the calmer he/she is. You need to practice some form of strength training regularly and make it part of your life.

Closing Thoughts

What can I say to sum everything up? Life can be hard. Life can be rough. But stress builds character, as they say. And I totally agree. Learn to embrace instability, learn to be free. It's all in your head. No need to make excuses not to train. On the other hand, no need to worry that you are not training as often and as much as you like. It's a good thing. You learn to value training. It becomes much more precious practice. And despite its importance, training shouldn't be a thing that takes away all your time.

THE MAIN BENEFIT OF STRENGTH TRAINING

You should know that strength training is a powerful tool. I am brave enough to say that *strength training is the most powerful tool every human has in his arsenal*. I love it and everything that is connected. It has tons of applications. Do you want to get strong? Try strength training. Do you want to build muscle? Try strength training. Do you want to get ripped? Have you heard about strength training? Strength is the key to everything. You need strength. You are nothing without it. And you are everything if you have it.

Strength training teaches you many things. For example, how to get good, and eventually great at something. Take Dave Tate's "Shit-Suck-Good-Great" scheme as an example. At first, you are "Shit". It does not matter what you deal with: training, business, drawing, or playing musical instruments, etc. At first you not even "Suck", you are "Shit". You cannot press an empty bar or squat with it, you cannot do even one Pull-Up, etc. It is the breaking point. You either push through it, or quit (of course, with some lame excuse like "well, it's not mine" or "I have no talent").

If you did the right thing and pushed through, you get to the "Suck" stage. You are not "Shit" anymore, but not "Good" either. Some people stay on this level with the comfortable thought that they just "keep themselves in shape". However, we all know (and they know it too) that they are just weak little pussies that are afraid to take a step further. You know whom I am talking about - the "I-don't-want-to-lift-heavy and I-don't-want-to-bulk-up guys and girls". Or the "you-don't-need-strength" type of trainees that look and perform like crap. In addition, you can put into this category all those pseudo-gurus and "it's-all-about-supplements" gym rats. They can spend countless hours arguing what exercise activates the lower pecs and rear delts more than actually training. That is why they suck.

If you did everything right, you get to the "Good" stage. You have decent levels of strength and mastery. All the "Suck" dudes are jealous and crying in their pillows all night long praying to get to your level. And here's another breaking point. You need to decide whether you want to achieve "Great" so bad that you will make necessary sacrifices or not. You have no guarantees that you will reach it, but if you dedicate yourself to achieving it, you will. Once you get to "Great" stage though, there will still be room for improvement.

What does this example show us? Strength training teaches us how to conquer our goals progressively. From "Shit" to "Great". Strength training teaches us to embrace patience. It teaches us that you need to make sacrifices to get something valuable. It teaches us respect and humbleness.

Despite the importance of these lessons, none of them is the main benefit of strength training in my opinion.

So What Is the Main Benefit of Strength Training?

Confidence? Yes, but that is also not the main one. The main benefit of strength training is the incredible mental strength to overcome difficulties. You will rarely find an article on this theme on the Internet. Why? Because all that matters to people today is looks. Everybody wants to be big or ripped, or both. Nobody cares about strength. And even less people care about mental strength. This is wrong.

Just imagine what the world would look like if there were many mentally strong people out there. I think it would be definitely better. What do we have now? People that are afraid to make decisions, parents that abandon their children, men that beat women, women that act like whores, everybody finds relaxation and eventually meaning of life in alcohol and drugs. This all comes from mental weakness.

Nobody has insurance from crappy things and situations in life. They will happen. However, strength training builds qualities that help to overcome those bad things. That is the main benefit of strength training. That is enough. Now it is time for you to get incredibly strong. Not only on the outside, but also on the inside.

RANDOM THOUGHTS

13 RANDOM TIPS ON ROUGH STRENGTH TRAINING

Sometimes it takes only one tip from another person (usually a person with a well-developed common sense) to turn on the switch in your head. Have you ever been in such situation? You struggle to find the best solution for your problem. You read all the available literature. You get a severe headache from endless thinking and researching. Your eyes fall out of sockets, but everything is in vain. Suddenly it takes only one word from the right person and everything gets into its right place in your head.

Here is an example. Some time ago I was analyzing all possible ways to make my own weighted vest filled with sand, while simultaneously driving myself crazy with all the ideas. Then in one conversation on this subject, my friend told me the simplest thing: "Hey! Why don't you use a backpack?" I was like: "But it won't work for this and that". However, a bit later I came to conclusion that a backpack will do the trick for almost every exercise that I need.

As you can see, any tip can give you some enlightenment. Therefore, here are my 13 random tips on rough strength training:

1. Avoid muscular failure.

This one is simple. Everybody knows about it. However, more and more people train on the edge of their current possibilities. That's not right, in my opinion. The more you drain your nervous system, the more time you will need to recuperate, therefore, you will be able to train less frequently. The consequences of muscle failure contradict with the simplest law of strength training: "Train as frequently as possible, while staying as fresh as possible". Strength is a skill, and you need to develop it as one. We will talk more about it in tip #2.

There are times when muscular failure is suitable. For example, a powerlifting contest, a strongman competition, the Olympics, etc.

However, if you are not fighting for medals, then leave your ego at the door. Use the intensity that is appropriate for YOU. I have seen lots of guys screw up big time because of their impatience. They get injured as fast as possible, instead of getting strong ASAP. I was a victim of impatience myself. Sometimes I still am. It never goes away. You need to tame your ego EVERY training session. Unless you want to hit a plateau sooner, get injured, and have no progress.

I should note that training to muscular failure can be useful in bodybuilding. Plenty of trainees have implemented it with success. However, I highly doubt that their joints are happy, especially past their forties.

Finally, by "muscular failure" here I mean a situation when you cannot resist the weight on its way down (in other words, it is muscular failure in the negative phase). You know, when the guy seems to be doing a Bench Press, but in reality his spotter does an Upright Row. In my opinion, this is unacceptable in proper strength training. On the other hand, muscular failure in the positive phase *can be applied* to get results, but remember that it is much more demanding than to leave one or two reps in the tank.

2. If you want to get good at something, practice it more.

If you want to learn guitar, you won't play it only once a week, right? You will be practicing daily. The same is true for strength. However, there is one difference. Strength training drains your energy resources a lot more comparing to playing the guitar or riding a bike. That is why you will not be able to practice it that often. This fact aside, the rules remain the same. The more often you practice a skill, the better you get at it.

I should note here that not all practice is useful. Consider the fact that to get good, you repeat the same thing over and over. Here is where the quality of your practice comes to play. The body does not realize on its own whether your technique is optimal or crappy. It is just trying to adapt to the stimulus. With repetition, it will get used to certain form. Your goal is to make your practice as perfect as possible for the body to absorb the best technique at initial stages. There are exceptions, but it is better to learn proper form at the beginning than to correct it later.

Here is another thing on frequent practice. What I want to emphasize is the importance of manipulating training volume, intensity, and frequency. You should understand by now that you cannot have everything together. If your intensity is high, frequency and volume suffer. If your volume is high, then intensity and frequency should be lower. The main trick is to find that "sweet spot" that makes you progress the way you want.

Regarding this particular example (getting good through frequent practice), you should understand that if your goal is certain frequency (say, 6 days a week), then either intensity, or volume should go down. My advice would be to lower down the volume to a minimum (to leave intensity pretty high). Let's break down a viable example:

1. You want to squat 6 days a week.

2. You start with 1 set of 5 with 7RM 6 days a week. That's only 6 sets per week.

3. Next week you add 1-2 sets to your weekly volume. For example, Monday and Thursday would be 2 sets of 5 with the same weight.

4. In following 5-11 weeks add 1-2 sets until you reach 3 sets of 5 for 6 days a week.

5. Retest your 7-repetition maximum and start over with 1 set of 5 protocol and new weight.

It is simple and effective way to implement high frequency training into your routine. Of course, all the other leg work in the example above should be minimized.

3. Cut sugar completely for the next 30 days.

Let us get somewhat experimental. You should know by this time that sugar is far from perfect for your body. Everybody knows that. Nevertheless, some people just cannot imagine their life without "white death" (I did not plan to sound too dramatic, but I could not resist the urge to use this word combination). They were eating cakes and cookies all their life (that is why they are fat and ugly). One day they embrace the understanding of the importance of diet. Everybody wants to look better, no matter what they say. Instead of saying "goodbye" to sugar and sweets, they do many ineffective and sometimes stupid things. For example, shoving down the throat all the sugar they can before 6 PM with hope that metabolism is faster in the morning. Of course, this will not work, as well as eating fewer sweets but each and every day.

My solution to this problem is simultaneously radical and simple. Cut down all the sugar and sweets completely for the next 30 days. Will it be hard? I barely made it through first two weeks (I fucking love sweet stuff). However, by the end of week #3 I felt almost no addiction. After 30 days, I finally have the ultimate control over that sweet tooth.

The main trick here is the number 30. Thirty days are just a little bit more than 4 weeks. Give yourself a promise that you will be able to eat any amount of sweets after that period is over. In reality, you might not even want to eat those sweets in 30 days from now.

Defeating a sugar addiction is another strength and victory in your arsenal. Do not underestimate it. You will be leaner and healthier in the end. Besides, defeating sugar addiction is much easier than opiate one. You just cannot make excuses after the last sentence.

4. Get up earlier.

"In what universe is this connected to strength training? Are you my grandpa or what?" Hold on. Before you drop this idea as useless let me give you some food for thought. I will not tire you with all this circadian rhythms stuff. We both know that it takes some consistency and your day can become inverted. You know, getting up in the evening and going to bed in the morning/afternoon. If you can sustain this type of a day, your biological rhythms adjust and there is almost no difference, except one…

Of course, it all depends on the individual, and my daytime patterns probably will not fit another person, but 95% of the time that I wake up later, I feel like crap. My eyes will not open without a decent dose of caffeine. It takes at least an hour more to get into my usual focused state. And after dusk I still have a feeling that the most productive part of the day is over. So it boils down to common sense.

If I wake up at 7-9 AM:
- I feel focused in an hour;
- I finish all my writing and editing for the day earlier;
- I create and adjust programs for clients earlier;
- I have much more time to create my music [18];
- I have time to train twice a day;
- I have more free time
- I have more energy throughout the day etc.

If I wake up at 12 AM – 1 PM, I can easily subtract 4-5 hours from my day, considering that evening most of the time feels unproductive to me.

I encourage you to try getting up earlier and decide whether it is your thing or not. I experienced a dramatic increase in productivity when I implemented this. Of course, if you are a loner and rarely have contact with other people, there are far better methods of increasing productivity. For example, the one I learnt from Tim Ferriss' "4-Hour Body". This method proves that you can be fully recovered sleeping only 2 hours per day. You should split them into six 20-minute naps and spread them evenly throughout the day. For more information read the book. The only downside of this method – your social life will suffer big time. But there is always price to pay.

Finally, yes, I can use an alarm if I am not sure that I will get up early. Do not be afraid to use it. An alarm is a good solution for productivity.

5. Even the toughest of us have bad days.

You may think that all the big guys (in any area of life) have no bad days. You may think that every training session of the coaches and athletes you follow is comprised of endless PRs. However, the reality is opposite. The more mature you get in terms of training experience, the less great sessions you have. Everything gets tougher and tougher. The thing that will differentiate the good athlete from the great is the ability to overcome endless failures.

Sometimes it feels like you are hitting the wall with your head. However, a chain of pathetic training sessions may lead to a PR. You never know. Importantly, you should analyze everything you do and check if you are not actually wasting your time. Assuming you have started a training log, I suggest you to compare not just training sessions in one mesocycle, but data from several mesocycles, and even macrocycles. This will keep you sane and more objective. In times when you feel that your training is moving nowhere, it is great to see where you have been 3, 6, 12 months ago. Unless, of course, you have done more in that time.

My point here is that everybody has bad days. And the better you get at something, the more crappy moments you'll have. You either get comfortable with failures, or forget about achieving anything great.

How to get comfortable with failures? Chances are that you never will. However, here are couple of tips:

- Appreciate those who support you. Treat them like gold. These people will give you energy to move on.
- Always strive to improve. Never stop. Educate yourself every day.
- Analyze your mistakes and never repeat them.

6. If you a hit plateau, change something.

There is no point in doing something again and again if you see no results. You will hit a plateau in all exercises eventually. If you never experienced this, then you either not consistent enough, or are at the beginner stage where you can progress for several months in a row without changing a thing.

There is nothing wrong with hitting plateaus, except the feeling of frustration. It is an essential part of the process for strength training (as well as any other area of life). Your body adapts to the stimulus and the regimen stops working. Despite what other people say, you need variety. Your body demands it. The best thing you can do when you hit a plateau is to change something. Even subtle changes can lead to progress.

However, variety can be different. You can implement it the right way or the wrong way.

Wrong ways:
- You change exercises and routines every training session;
- You drop one exercise completely to work on another;
- When you get back to a certain exercise, you are much weaker.

Right ways:
- Changes are subtle. You stay focused on your goals;
- You don't drop an important exercise, you put it into maintenance mode;
- When you get back to a certain exercise, you are at least at the same level, if not stronger.

In other words, variety should supercharge your training, not spoil it. Let us break down an example. You are a regular fitness enthusiast and your Bench Press has stalled.

- You can change the set/rep scheme. If you were doing 5×5, switch to 3×3 or 4×6.

- You can drop down the intensity and work your way up again. If you were pressing 100 kg for 5×5, lower the working weight to 85 kg and progress in small increases again.

- You can change exercises. For example, to the Dumbbell Bench Press, Floor Press, Paused Bench Press etc. However, you should be careful. Some exercises do not have the carryover. Still you will never know until you try. Even the slightest change can give results. For example, changing to a slightly inclined Bench Press.

If you participate in a sport like powerlifting, then you should understand that changing exercises completely is not an option. However, introducing variety through assistance work is totally viable.

In addition, it seems that every gym maggot likes to use "the Bulgarians" to prove that variety is not important. Here is my little note to those people. Firstly, if you have not actually trained with Bulgarians of that era, it is just speculation. Secondly, working to the maximum lift for the particular day is the ultimate variety, isn't it? You rarely work with the same weight.

Take-home point: variety works when implemented properly. Stop wasting your time.

7. Get outdoors.

Yep. Right now. Go for a walk. Breathe some fresh air. It is essential for your brain function. Get outdoors every day. Do not spend all your time in front of the black mirror. A 30-minute walk everyday can improve the quality of your life tremendously. It will clear your head and get you energized. I go for a walk every morning. It is the perfect time.

Maybe it is nothing new for you, but I have noticed that training outdoors is far superior than indoors. Let me give you an example. Usually when I sleep less than 6-7 hours, my training sessions suck. No matter what I do. No dose of caffeine can fix that. However, when I train outside, it does not matter. It seems that fresh air can improve my strength in suboptimal circumstances. This may also be true for you. If you are sleep-deprived for some reason and need to train, then try to do it outside. Let me know how it worked.

There is only one temporary downside of the outdoors training. You may lose some strength during the first sessions because of the new environment. Everything will feel new to you and your body. However, in 2-3 sessions you will regain all your strength.

8. Use both low and high reps.

There are many debates on what is cooler – low reps or high? The right answer is both. Both of them have pluses and minuses.

Low reps (1-5) are great for building strength and learning new more demanding exercise variations. They are not optimal for building muscle when done with really high intensity. Hypertrophy requires volume. If you do 1-7 total reps, you might not experience it at all. Additionally, you can get into a common low-rep trap when you decrease training volume to continue increasing intensity. You go from 5×5 to 3×3, to 3×2, to 2×1 etc. While this is usable, I would not recommend doing it often. Your nervous system will not take too much of this.

High reps (8-12) are great for hypertrophy and strength-endurance. However, they will not help with developing maximal strength.

So here's the thing. If you want more strength and muscle, you need to implement both rep ranges in your training. They both control each other. High reps will tell you when you are working too hard, while low reps will identify when you are wasting time by training too easy.

How does this work? The classic way to use both rep ranges is to put strength work first and hypertrophy second. Here is example upper body workout:

A1) Bench Press 3×3
A2) Weighted Pull-Ups 3×3
B1) Ring Dips 4×8
B2) Sandbag Bent-Over Rows 4×8

Additionally, with calisthenics you will not be able to progress in actual 3×3 or 4×8. That is where this repetition cross-section (5-8) comes really handy. When you cannot progress from current exercise to the next one, work up not to 5 reps, but to 8-10. This should make the transition much smoother.

9. One step at a time.

This is important in any area of life. Especially if you are impatient type of person and have nobody to ask. Chances are that you have made this mistake before (and repeatedly).

Every novice trainee wants to have it all and at once. He wants big muscles, a ripped body, maybe lots of strength, great grip, etc. In some time (after watching YouTube), he might want to add One-Arm Handstands, solid Olympic lifting, bouldering, sandbag training, kettlebell training, and the Iron Cross to the mix. His diet should be perfect (does it really exist?); he buys all the supplements he can afford. In the end, of course, he drops training in 2-4 weeks. What is the problem?

You cannot have all at once. To get results, training and diet should be your habits, not some temporary tools. The best way to nurture a habit is to make the smallest change to your current regimen. The above fitness enthusiast could have made it much better if he concentrated just on 3 exercises: Pull-Ups, Push-Ups (or Dips) and Squats. That is it. How do you think what is more sustainable: trying to gain all at once or just training 3 exercises 2-3 times per week? I think the answer is obvious.

The more complicated approach you take, the less chances you have to win. Do you want to learn the Handstand? Do not start with the freestanding one. The only thing that is waiting for you in this case is frustration. Start with the simplest thing you can do. Go from Wall-Assisted Headstands, Wall-Assisted Handstands, Crow Stands, etc. Train it 2-3 times per week. That is attainable by anyone. Progress from there.

The same is true for any area of life you want to improve. Do you want to read great books, but don't have time? Devote 1 hour a week to this. It is easy. With time, you will understand that you can read every day, and you will be accomplishing your goal.

Do you want to learn to play the guitar? Start with the most basic exercises 2-3 hours per week. In couple of months, you will be nailing some simple stuff.

Besides, when you make only one change, it is much easier to concentrate on it. And it becomes your habit much faster.

10. Don't neglect mobility/flexibility training.

If you have great flexibility, then skip this tip and know that I hate you. My mobility/flexibility always sucked. It sucked so hard that Sasha Grey would be jealous. It never bothered me though. Strength in the gym was always great. However, when I started this handbalancing thing, I understood all the importance of flexibility.

Let me explain and reveal the dark truth. If you ever plan to nail a One-Arm Handstand and your flexibility sucks, forget about it. Yes, you can reach a regular Handstand with poor flexibility. You can make it somewhat straighter, but it is far from what you will require. In addition, forget about Press Handstands and lots of advanced handbalancing.

Is it possible to reach high-level positions with poor mobility? Yes, if you are lightweight and very lucky. Yet I would not put all my stakes on sheer luck.

What to do? For handbalancing and gymnastic skills in particular, you will need to address several areas:
- Shoulders
- Lats
- Pecs
- Hips

- Hamstrings

To determine what you need to work on, you should make some flexibility tests:

1. You can find a comprehensive shoulder flexibility test here [19].

2. You should be able to touch your knees with your head in the pike position. Your knees should be locked. If you cannot, then probably your hamstrings are shortened.

3. You should be able to perform front splits with both sides, as well as side splits.

If you meet all the criteria, then all you need is strength. If not, then you should master those positions as soon as possible.

11. Protein.

Do you know what is the simplest diet change you can make today to get all the results you want? No, it is not cutting gluten, not fearing carbs, not low-fat nonsense, not intermittent fasting (although I love it), and certainly not veganism. The most simple and powerful thing you can do is to concentrate on protein. Yep, that is it. I said this before; I will say it again. Count actual protein grams. Shoot for at least 2-3 g per kilogram of your bodyweight. Do not worry about other things. Just do this.

How are you supposed to do it? If you eat packaged food, usually you can find nutritional facts on the back of the product. If you eat real food, then use any reliable calorie counter or Google. Add the entire amount you have eaten throughout the day and be amazed how little it is.

If your weight is 85 kg, you will need 170-255 g of protein per day with the sweet spot at 212.5 g. Of course, all numbers are free for interpretation. You may need to go up to 300 g; and I would not go lower than 170 g.

Some people are good with low amounts of protein. Those bastards can eat what they want and be ripped and muscular. But for the vast majority of losers like us, see-it-eat-it approach wouldn't work. Count protein and get less fat and more muscular. Unless you want to remain fat, weak, and lame.

12. Good programming = finding what works for you.

People always tend to look for the best approach for someone else. They look for the *exact things* other people did to get results. While modeling successful dudes and dudettes is a great thing, doing exactly what they did is often a recipe for failure. What you need to understand is the fact that you must *find what works for you* applying *the principles of successful people*, not blindly repeating what works for them. Exact programs of champions will not work for you, unless you have the same genetics and conditions. However, the principles of progressive resistance, manipulating volume, intensity and frequency, and concentrating on big compound lifts will work.

Different coaches will tell you different things. All of them are right to some extent. Still no matter what this or that coach says (except me, of course), if that doesn't work for you, then drop it. If it works, then remember what you did (or better write it down).

Your goal should be to collect all the techniques that work for you and to apply them. They may change with time, but most of them will remain current forever.

Here are several things that work for me:
- Handstand training should be frequent;
- If I work hard, I'll need a week of rest;
- I can train the same muscle groups with different exercises throughout the week;
- I rarely can train same muscle groups the next day;
- If I cannot repeat the result of previous session on the first set, it is better to rest.

13. Keep it simple.

Simplicity is the ultimate sophistication. You may want to keep your programs and diet complex, but in reality, they shouldn't be so. It is just the opposite of that. The more variables you have in your approach, the less results you get. Here is a simple equation analogy. What will be easier to solve: an equation with only one variable or several? The answer is obvious. The same is true for strength training and diet.

Chances are that you heard about the Pareto principle or 80/20 law. Only 20% of your activities give you 80% of results. This simple concept can be applied to any area of life. You will not believe how accurate it is. Apply this law whenever you are in doubt. If your training gets too complicated, define what 20% of exercises give you the most bang for the buck. If your diet is too sophisticated, then find that 20% (reread the protein tip again).

Keep it simple and start acquiring those damn gains.

THE TOP 5 EXERCISES FOR AWESOME SHOULDER DEVELOPMENT

You may wonder why the fuck do I write an article on such trendy and obvious thing. Hell, you can search the internet and there will be tons of info on shoulder training. And I am cool with it. However, I would like to write the Rough Strength version. It is the sum of my own training experience. Besides, there are lots of people who are new to training, and they are wondering how to get those strong cannonball shoulders.

Why am I writing about shoulders? Why not legs? Why not biceps and abs? It is because shoulders are the most masculine part of the body (along with traps). Nothing will make you stand out from the crowd like well-developed shoulders. The shoulder is one of the most complex joints, so it is wise to develop them. In addition, if you noticed, all the upper body movement patterns are based on the shoulder position.

So here are the Rough Strength top 5 exercises for awesome shoulder development:

5. Sandbag Military Press

In fifth place, is the Sandbag Military Press. You can see the photos of start and finish positions of the exercise on the next page.

Basic technique points are:
- Keep your glutes and abs tight;
- When you press the bag overhead, try to press it back, behind your head. This will ensure that you press it straight up;
- Lock the elbows at every rep;
- Always touch the chest at the bottom.

Why do I like the Sandbag Military Press for shoulder development? I like this movement for its functionality. It teaches you to lift over your head an unstable always-changing object. It builds shoulder and triceps strength not many exercises will be able to match. I highly recommend you to use this exercise in training routine if your goal is maximal upper body strength and size development.

4. Kettlebell Seated Press

Kettlebell Seated Press is number 4. Look at the pictures for the beginning and end positions of this exercise:

I will try to explain it too. It is simple and effective. You take a seat on the floor. Take the kettlebell in one hand. Then press it overhead without holding anything with the other hand. You will notice that your shoulders get fried with much less weight compared to the Military Press. It happens because you cannot use your legs and lower back. Your shoulders work much more in this exercise. Why unilateral? Because there is a big chance that you will fall if you press two kettlebells. If you are brave, you can do it bilateral.

This exercise will be like breath of fresh air when your Military Presses will stall. In addition, the Kettlebell Sots Press can be in this category too.

3. Planche Push-Ups

Planche Push-Ups (as well as the static Planche) would be number 3. Despite the fact that most of the trainers will put Planche Push-Ups in "horizontal push", it works slightly different muscles than classic exercises from this category. The Bench Press, for example, works mostly pectoral muscles with some shoulder and triceps involvement (for different people the level of involvement will be different). Planche Push-Ups on the other hand, work mostly shoulder muscles and lats. Chest muscles and triceps do not get as much work to do as in Bench Press. Anyway, this exercise is awesome for shoulder development and you cannot deny it. Hell, you are holding your body parallel to the ground and doing Push-Ups in this position. Your shoulders get a lot of action (ranging from stabilization to dynamic movement).

Here are the pictures of the bottom and top positions (I know that the elbows are not fully locked at the top; it is work in progress):

You will definitely want to add these bad boys to your training regimen. However, here is a word of advice for you. Do not force your progress because it will not come faster. Stay with the tuck version as long as it takes to master it. Do not be a fool. The Planche is not a skill that you will be able to obtain overnight. Be prepared for several years of hard work. In the end, it will be well worth it.

2. Clean & Press

Number 2 is the clean and press. It is classic exercise that gets forgotten all the time. Why do you want to clean the weight every rep? Because by doing so you will give your shoulders more work to do (especially the posterior deltoid). You will ensure good, well-balanced shoulder development, and a ton of usefulness as a side effect.

So the movement is composed of two parts: clean and press. The weight is on the floor. You come to it. Clean it. Press it. Lower it down. Repeat. Simple. Look at the photos in this section for guidance in this exercise:

You can do this exercise with any type of weight. Use barbell, dumbbells, kettlebells, sandbag, stone etc. Your fantasy is the limit. My preference would probably be kettlebells. Nevertheless, I like the Barbell Clean and Press too, as well as every other variation. It is just cool movement. Do it.

1. Handstand Push-Ups

And number one is, of course, the Handstand Push-Up and all its variations. I can go on and on talking about this exercise. So to save your time I only say that Handstands and Handstand Push-Ups are synonyms of awesome shoulder development. This includes all the variations: Handstands, Press Handstands, wall-assisted Handstand Push-Ups, freestanding Handstand Push-Ups, 90 Degree Push-Ups, Planche Presses to Handstands, etc. Why do I like it so much? Because all you need is your body and occasionally some wall. In addition, the benefits are tremendous. In the process of mastering this exercise, you will become the possessor of more stable and robust upper body.

In my opinion, Handstand Push-Ups are the best choice for shoulder (as well as upper body) development.

Exercises to Keep Your Shoulders Healthy

The exercises I mentioned are less harmful to your shoulder joints than everybody's favorite Bench Press, but, anyway, it's a good idea to develop rotator cuffs and overall shoulder health and mobility. Here are 2 ways to make it happen:

1. Cuban Press or Rotation

The most boring video ever [20], but very good exercise for shoulder and particularly rotator cuff health. What is the difference between press and rotation? In the Cuban Press, you *press* the weight up after the rotation and *lower* it fully between reps.

2. Scapula Mobilization by Ido Portal
It is very sound routine for scapula mobilization [21]. Use it.

And Don't Forget Pulling
It is always a good idea to balance out your pushing work with pulling. So when you construct your routine, do not concentrate blindly on pushing. Throw in some pulling like Pull-Ups, Front Lever Rows, Kettlebell Rows, High Pulls, Snatches, Cleans etc. Always try to maintain structural balance as much as possible. This way you will ensure that you will not get injuries.

Closing Thoughts
So there you have it. Rough Strength's version of top 5 exercises for awesome shoulder development. Use it wisely, and finally build some cannonball shoulders you will be able to crush walls with.

INTERVIEWS

POWER BAR TALK WITH EDWARD OF BARSTARZZ

Look at this man. This is Edward. He is the founder of the Barstarzz. I was lucky enough to interview him this morning (actually, it was the late evening in New York City). He trains exclusively with his own bodyweight. He is as strong as he looks. He performs amazing feats of strength, agility, balance etc. How this man was able to build such an amazing physique exclusively with his bodyweight? Because calisthenics work. And he's not the only one. Look at other BarStarzz's athletes. They look AND perform totally awesome. It's not genetics. It's consistency and perseverance. These things build such great strength and such great bodies. I'm really sick and tired of people that say something like "Oh! I need a gym membership to become strong and fit" or "Oh! I don't have time to train". Seriously? Forget your excuses and go train! How can you train with your own bodyweight, get superstrong and achieve such an amazing body? Read on.

Hi, Edward! How you doing? Tell us about BarStarzz.

Hi, Alex. BarStarzz is a fitness organization that's international. We've come together to push forward the idea that you can train your body, gain strength and definition, without ever stepping in a gym. Just at your local park or at home with very minimum equipment. And hopefully we just trying to spread the message to people through our videos. And now we are going through a stage where we're showing 'how to'. So we're showing you what to eat now, what workouts to perform.

Very interesting. What can you tell us about your workouts?

I work out strictly through calisthenics, so I really use no weight lifting, no traditional [implements like] dumbbells or barbells. I wake up and I go to the park. So I do a lot of different pull-ups, push-ups, dips. I try a lot of different moves. I like to experiment with my creativity. [I try to] do as much as I can with all the equipment I have.

Ok. And how would your typical workout look like?

That's hard to say because I switch my routines out daily. I always have different stuff to do. That's why I can't stick to one routine. You want to shock your body so your muscles will continue growing. And you don't want to get bored of workouts. We always make up games, we try to beat each other's score in pull-ups or would go back and forth with different tricks. But I never stick to one particular routine 'cause then I go crazy. I want to have the fun that I have from doing this.

I have a long workout. So I would say I work out a good hour and a half to two hours. Sometimes even more. I get together with a group of friends, and we go to a park. It's usually afternoon. It's the best time for me. We choose the workout routine once we get there, you know. Once I get there, I start thinking and whatever I'm in the mood to do that day we start to do it. Or someone else can take charge and they say what to do. So we all take charge giving our routines and we just try them.

Do you train daily?

I train about 5-6 days a week. You have to build up to it. It took me awhile. When I first started working out, I worked out 1 day and 1 day off. Over time my body got more and more used to it and I made it to workouts 5-6 days in a row.

I think it's the most asked boring question, but anyway. Can you gain muscle mass with calisthenics?

Yeah, you definitely can. I'm a big dude, you know. I'm not huge, but I have like about 17 inch (43.1 cm) arms or 18 inch (45.7 cm). Around there. A lot of people consider it big. And all I do is calisthenics. So you definitely can get big from calisthenics. Before I started working out I was real skinny and real small. Not anymore.

Do you perform leg work?

Yes. I do a lot of sprinting up and down stairs. I also perform a lot of pistols and jumping squats because I like to work on my explosive jump, so I'm doing a lot of plyometrics, when it comes to my legs, of course, using bodyweight.

When you train your pull-ups, dips and push-ups do you prefer lots of volume or you pick more challenging variations?

I do both. Like I said, I'm more into creativity, trying different stuff and mixing stuff together. So one day I do a lot of pull-ups and I go for numbers. And the next day, you know, I work on one-arm pull-ups or stuff that is harder and I won't be able to do as much reps. But just to keep me entertained.

What more can you say about calisthenics?

I think a lot of people are confused when it comes to calisthenics. They think that it's only a good way to get ripped, or [that] it's not as good as bodybuilding, or lifting weights, but it definitely worked a lot for me and a lot for other people. It's a great thing, you know. You are able to work out and get a great workout paying nothing, you able to get just as big as the guys in the gym, if not stronger. Because this stuff I've seen done in the park I've never seen done in the gym.

Yeah! I've seen a lot of good squatters or good deadlifters, or good bench pressers that can't even do a pull-up or a couple of push-ups.

I've seen a lot of such guys. When I used to go to the gym, there used to be a lot of guys that are really big and they could bench a lot. You know, they could go heavy on the weights, but when it came to doing pull-ups they perform with bad form and reps of 5. I think the most important thing that you can do when it comes to fitness is to get acquainted with your bodyweight. You should be able to do everything with your bodyweight.

Do you perform grip work?

Just recently I started playing around with using two-finger pull-ups, finger push-ups and finger planches. But as far as actual gripping, I don't perform any gripping exercises.

What about gymnastics?

Yeah, I definitely practice a lot of gymnastic moves. But I don't like to practice just plain gymnastic moves. I practice it, but I always like to add my own little twist to it. It wouldn't be a regular back lever, it would be a back lever where I move my legs side-to-side or something, you know. I like to add my own little twist to everything I do.

Have you experienced elbow tendonitis?
I think everyone I know who trains with calisthenics experienced it at one point. You will experience it with time no matter what you're doing. When you get it just relax the body part that hurts from it. And when you rest, ice it three times a day. Icing really helps. Remember to warm-up before working out and to stretch after. Doing these steps will prevent tendonitis or at least help to treat it better.

Any interesting stuff about BarStarzz?
We came on news couple of times. Right now we're working on a DVD. We want to tell people exactly how to learn how to do a lot of different moves that we do, to speak on diet, to speak on a lot of different stuff that people unsure on fitness. We all come together to make this DVD. And now we are about to come out with a new YouTube channel on Spanish for all our Spanish followers.

What countries do BarStarzz include?
Right now it's America, Bulgaria, and Italy. But we're looking forward to spreading it to more countries. The thing is, I like to be really involved with people that represent us. You got to make sure that they are positive people and are spreading the same message.

Ok. You've mentioned diet. What are your views on it?
My diet: I don't eat any diary or any grains for 6 days out of the week. And then one day of the week I eat whatever I want. So during the week I eat something like tuna, eggs, chicken, beans, natural peanut butter, a lot of different fruits and vegetables. That's mostly what I eat during the week. Also a lot of eggs. And one day of the week I eat whatever I'm craving. I try to get protein in every one of my meals throughout of the day. I eat between 4 to 5 times a day including snacks (fruit shakes or can of tuna).

Do you count calories?
No, not at all. I don't believe in counting calories. I think that was is more important is the quality of the food that you're eating.

Your advice to Rough Strength followers?
Start slow. You don't want to get injured. You definitely need to master the basics as far as pull-ups, push-ups, dips, squats, crunches, knee raises. Stick to the basics until you feel real comfortable with it. And then start moving on to harder stuff and start experimenting what works best for you. Remember, everyone has a different body. What works for somebody might not work for you. That's about it. Take your time.

Some closing thoughts?

I just hope everyone gets a chance to check us out on YouTube, Facebook, Twitter and the website. Keep expecting the YouTube videos on tutorials. Let us know what you want, so we can get out videos for you. Be patient. The DVD is on its way. Thank you, Alex, for the interview. [Alex: DVD is already out]

Thanks, Edward. It was nice talking to you. Keep up with your stuff.

INTERVIEW WITH THESUPERSAIYAN

Recently I was lucky enough to interview a guy who is a big inspiration for many people around the world, as well as for me. He calls himself TheSupersaiyan. He has developed pretty decent levels of strength and mastery in calisthenics. So let's dive into this interview.

AZ: Hi, Vass! Tell our readers about yourself.

TheSupersaiyan: Hey, I'm 23 years old and I'm a great fan of feats of bodyweight strength as you can see from my videos. I love in particular everything related to planches and handstands. Pushing movements are my favorites including all variations of planche push-ups, handstand push-ups, one arm handstands and so on. However, I also like pulling movements such as front lever, one arm pull up, back lever, and everything that is practiced on gymnastic rings. I want to be the most multi-purpose athlete I can be. My goal is to become as strong as I can, to do things that nobody has done before, and get superhuman strength. Become the legendary supersaiyan :)

AZ: Ok, so how did you get started with strength training? How long have you been doing it?

TheSupersaiyan: I watched some videos back in early 2008 on YouTube. They were videos from Bartendaz and Zakaveli (Zef from Bar-Barians now), at that time there was nobody but them on YouTube. And I was impressed by what they were doing; it motivated me to do the same. So I started trying to do the movements like them and I loved working out outdoors. But at that time I was not yet focused on strength as I'm now, but this is how I started practicing barhitting (street workout). I started to focus my training on strength around September 2008 after some months of training, I wanted to do harder moves such as the planche and handstand pushups so at this time I started my strength training. I started 4 years ago but I really did like 3-3.5 years of training or something.

AZ: Interesting. Describe your training style.

TheSupersaiyan: Well, it's quite simple, my training is focused towards advanced gymnastic moves. On strength, so I do most of time sets of a few reps with long rest between sets. Sometimes, I do not follow my training program and I train according to my wishes of the day depending on my energy levels that day, it's good for the mind from time to time. Most of the time I follow my weekly training routine. I do from time to time some strength/endurance training, but most of time it is focused on pure strength. I never do training based on muscular endurance, such as exercises with long sets above 15 reps with short rest. The easiest pushing movement of my training is a freestanding handstand push-up and the easiest pulling movement is front lever. I only do the basic stuff such as pushups, dips or pull-ups for warming up my body.

AZ: Well, your training style is quite like mine! Low rep strength stuff. It's awesome. Tell us more about your SuperSaiyan Requirements?

TheSupersaiyan: I'm glad you speak about them :) Dragon Ball Z gave me so much motivation that I decided to create my own supersaiyan requirements. Why? It's because it forces me to keep training hard while aiming for a high and difficult goal to advance from level to level. Having goals is the key to success, but having extremely difficult goals will take you much further. I love the conquest of power and strength in DBZ; from level to level goku trains harder and harder in order to become stronger and more ripped. This is the mindset I love, the conquest of strength. The Supersaiyan 4 requirement is very very hard to reach, it takes many years of hard work and dedication. Only the most dedicated and passionate people will reach it one day, because of the love of your passion you'll do any sacrifices needed to reach your goal. It's even above Olympic gymnastic level, about certain exercises. This way you know directly who is very dedicated or not and will get my respect. Many people ask me why there are no leg exercises. Because I don't want to put my effort, my sweat into leg exercises. I train them but it's not something I really like, it's only to keep a body proportioned, harmonious. I don't have any goal in this area and I focus on upper body strength only. This is totally personal, but each one acts according to his goals. Some people already achieved certain of my Supersaiyan requirements, I'm glad they have taken them as goals, but I would like to see more people interested about them. People may find them too hard, or they don't like some exercices I've put in them, but as I told, you can take inspiration and create yours then. So I thank you again for speaking about them :)

AZ: No problem, bro. What are your current training goals?

TheSupersaiyan: My current short term training goals are the One arm handstand, Hollow back, Maltese and, of course, reach my SS4 requirement.

AZ: What is the most important benefit of strength training, in your opinion?

TheSupersaiyan: Whatever your goal is, getting strong is the first thing to do. Once you're super strong, all doors are opened to you. You have no limit; this is the best benefit of strength training. It's like school, once you get the best diploma, you can go where you want. Here's the same. Being strong will help you with everything, even if your goals are based on muscular endurance such as 50 pull ups in a row. Being able to do a one arm pull up will help towards this goal, but the reverse is not necessarily (*so true! - Alex*). Like doing planche push ups will help you to do many regular push up easily, but someone able to do 200 push up will not have necessarily the strength to do a planche push up, and so on... Same about power, in order to be very powerful you need to be first super strong, $P = fv$.

Strength is the key for everything (*these are words of gold - Alex*).

AZ: What are your thoughts on nutrition?

TheSupersaiyan: Well, not much, I always eat according to my hunger. I eat healthy, lot of fruits, vegetables. Meat at every meal, chicken, beef, pork, eggs, turkey etc... I only drink water and milk throughout the day, rarely fruit juices. I prefer to eat my fruits. I also eat everything like pizza, hamburgers, or any other unhealthy food that everyone likes, but it's from time to time. I never deprive myself to eat anything. The only thing I care is to eat enough of protein per day and then I eat the carbs according to my hunger. That's it.

AZ: Are calisthenics popular in your country? Because here in Ukraine I see more and more people doing "Street Workout" stuff.

TheSupersaiyan: Well, not much for now, but it's growing well. Lot of projects are in progress. There is a competition called "King of Pull and Push." This year was the second time. Zef and Hit were there. This is a famous competition now :) I could not go, but I'll be there next time.

AZ: Some words of wisdom and advice for Rough Strength readers.

TheSupersaiyan: Think seriously about what you want the most. Do not train without goals. Set up goals and work hard to reach them. You can do anything you want. We are built the same way. It all depends on your motivation, dedication and rigor. There is no place for excuses. Do not even try, it's for cowards. As long as you believe in yourself, you'll be unstoppable. The only barrier between you and your dreams is your determination to achieve them. Do not let anybody tell you who you are and what you can or can't do. Your limits are in your mind, they don't really exist, clean your mind of all these bad thoughts. It's the first thing you must do, and it will stop you from doing anything in your life whatever the area. Do not compare yourself to anybody else, it's a waste of time, focus on your own progression and become better day after day. You can be better than many people, but if you can't beat yourself, well, you waste your time... It's the best way to stay motivated, take inspiration and motivation from other people. Do not envy them. Also do not forget to enjoy your training. If you do not like what you do, you won't go really far.

AZ: Ok, thank you for your time, Vass. It was very interesting to interview you. One last question: how people can find out more about you?

TheSupersaiyan: My facebook page: https://www.facebook.com/pages/TheSupersaiyan/188543874537883

MASTER KETTLEBELLS AND DUMBBELLS – INTERVIEW WITH YAHONT

I'm proud to present you an exclusive interview with a strongman and my fellow countryman Yahont. This man is inspirational. Now you are able to read his story and to know the principles that lie behind his training. And you know what? The main principles are the same: consistency, determination, and perseverance. Are you interested? Then read on.

Hi, Yahont! How you doing? Tell us more about yourself.

Hi, Alex. I started training in 2005. At first it was swimming and stuff. The next two and a half years I trained with a dumbbell. It was basic exercises: curl and press. The dumbbell was 7,5 kg at first, then 16 kg. I did high reps. I always strove to lift a heavier dumbbell. I couldn't go beyond 45 kg that time. With time, I changed my training protocol to lower reps. From the beginning of 2007 my approach to training and physical culture became more serious. I started using 8 sets of 5 reps. By the way, I started training with kettlebells in 2008. So there is an infinite struggle for me on what to choose for my training - kettlebells or dumbbells? Now I want to break new PRs with a dumbbell, for example. I still will be training with kettlebells. I will be doing Kettlebell Double Front Squats, Kettlebell Cleans, and maybe Kettlebell Double Military Presses and Kettlebell Double Push Presses periodically. I probably would be doing Bench Press and One-Arm Push

Press with a dumbbell. I would be striving for 6-8 reps.

What's the difference between kettlebells and dumbbells in your opinion?

Dumbbells provide you with skills that kettlebells cannot and vice versa. For example, to lift a stone you need strong wrists. Dumbbells strengthen the wrists. This is the advantage of dumbbells compared to kettlebells. Dumbbells provide full range of motion. For example, there is a difference between a kettlebell press and dumbbell press. A kettlebell is easier at the start because it's resting on your forearm. Use a slight motion and it's moving. With dumbbells it's different. You hold a dumbbell just in your hand at the start. That's why working with dumbbells may be actually heavier.

However, if you don't work with kettlebells it will be the opposite situation. Kettlebell lifting requires skills. That's why by combining kettlebell and dumbbell training you can acquire quite well-rounded strength in your arms and shoulders. Here's my observation. If you feel that you become weaker in dumbbell lifting, then you need to work with dumbbells. If you like to lift stones or sandbags, that would be better training with dumbbell. If you like to lift with both of your arms, then it's better to lift kettlebells rather than dumbbell because dumbbells weren't designed for this. I often see people take pair of dumbbells, take them to their shoulders and do half reps. That's not a press, it's a lockout. A press is a press. Imagine that you press a barbell. You need to press from your chest. Your hands need to be under your chin when you press. The same is true for kettlebells. When you press kettlebells from the position where they are resting on your shoulders you need just to straighten your arm a little bit and that's all. It's not a press if you do that.

What is heavy press? Here's Yahont pressing a pair of 50 kg kettlebells [22]

What are your tips on pressing?

You can't press a pair of kettlebells like a barbell. You need to bring your arms to sides. If you don't do this, then your elbows will hurt, and you won't be able to lockout the bells. The Kettlebell Double Military Press is very interesting and hard exercise. I was very interested in the Dumbbell One-Arm Press until 2010. Then I became very interested in the Kettlebell Double Military Press for maximum. It's interesting because maximum results in this exercise haven't been explored yet. Just look at powerlifting, Olympic weightlifting - you know the best results in different categories. However, the Kettlebell Double Military Press has not been explored. On the internet, there's only one video of the Englishman Rob Russel who push presses 60 and 48 kg kettlebells [23]. And his weight is 140 kg.

He probably could press a pair of 56 kg kettlebells for a single or double. I'm interested in developing pressing power for double press. I had a training session with the double press in 2010 with a pair of 44 kg kettlebells. I wasn't good at pressing 44's that time. So I pressed them for doubles. After the fifth or seventh set, I felt an uplift in energy. And I pressed them 5 times in the last set!

To become good at pressing a pair of kettlebells you need to clean them more frequently. You can face a problem in that you can press heavier bells, but can't clean them yet. When the total weight of the bells will be equal to your bodyweight, you will need decent power to clean them. You will need to train explosiveness to clean them. You can clean them either with a pre-swing or through explosiveness. You need to train explosiveness of legs, and it is trained well with dumbbell push presses. One more thing that I've noticed is that it's good to do front squats with kettlebells after dumbbell or kettlebell push presses. You take a heavy dumbbell or heavy kettlebell and push press it for 5 sets of 5 or 8 sets of 5.

I'd like to do an experiment. I haven't trained for 1,5 month due to disease. I will take a 54 kg dumbbell with thick handle (5 cm (2 inch)). I will do sets of 6 reps. And I will strive for 6 sets of 6. Then I will add reps to 6x7, then 6x8. I tried such training. It felt in my wrists. I had weaned off of dumbbell training. The next day I was sore in my shoulders. But it was a good, pleasant soreness. The next day I went to the beach and pressed an 80 kg stone overhead. And I couldn't press it earlier because of its awkwardness. When I worked with kettlebells this stone was "unpressable" for me. When I reintroduced dumbbell work to my training, I was able to press it. It's hard to push press a stone because it's awkward and has the form of a prism, but not ideal prism. When you clean it, one of its edges pushes right into your chin. Second thing is its center of gravity is off-axis. And when you press it, the stone tries either to fall forward or on your head. It's not a good idea to drop a stone on your head. It's not good for your health also. So the only way is press it up. When you press a kettlebell, your arm goes either forward or sideways. It doesn't straighten like if you take just your arm up. It's because of the center of gravity. And when you press a dumbbell your muscles work in a slightly different manner. The next thing is that you need to lower the weights down under control. It will prevent injuries.

So I should bother with dumbbell training?

Yes. If you don't have a dumbbell, you can buy a handle (or you can find a craftsman who will make a handle for you) where you will screw a pair of bolts into each side. Just look at my dumbbell [24].

It's very comfortable. If I use fewer plates, then I just take a shorter bolt. It's practical. If I need thicker handle, then I just switch handles. I have such set of handles: 37.5mm standard handle, a 50mm handle and a 62mm or 2.5-inch handle.

So you have a set of handles and just screw bolts on them, and put plates between the handle and bolts?

Yes, it's quite simple design. A set of handles, a pair of bolts and a set of plates is all that you need. You can adjust weight.

I saw that you have several methods of making kettlebells heavier on your livejournal. Tell us more.

You can make them adjustable with small dumbbells. Put small ropes on them.

When you use such adjustments, it's very quick. This way the weight isn't fixed. Look at photo below.

That's a pair of 45 kg kettlebells. The hanging dumbbells should be in the position like the one you see in the photo. There is one rule: when you hang a dumbbell on a kettlebell, it should be perpendicular to the handle. It's important. It should NOT hang parallel to the handle. This way of making kettlebells heavier is the quickest. It's even quicker than adjusting plates on a barbell. Other important thing is that you don't need to buy a whole set of kettlebells. You need just the basic kettlebells and a set of dumbbells with ropes. You can easily adjust your 32 kg kettlebells to 42 kg in two-arm work. But I had problems with cleaning two 48 kg kettlebells made such way.

I've seen you modified your sport-style 16 kg kettlebells with lead. Can you tell the story?

I had the following situation. One kettlebell became 46 kg and the second - 46.7 kg. Both are less than 48 kg. I placed a 2.4 kg plate on the bottom of one and 1.25 kg plate to another. That's how I have 48 kg kettlebells.

What exercise with kettlebells is beneficial in your opinion, except military presses, push presses, cleans?

Double Front Squats. Very hard exercise. Practice this exercise at least once a week. The Kettlebell Double Front Squat is as hard as the Kettlebell Double Military Press.

Do you perform any grip work?

No, not at all. Too much grip work, in my opinion, kills the desire to show results in basic exercises like the military press. And what's more important: good grip or a good military press? I think the answer is obvious. For me it's military press. You can power up your grip in months, but you can't make your military press stronger in such time.

I like the military press a lot, by the way

There's a problem with military press. It's better to train the military press with different assistance exercises like push presses and bench presses than with heavy military presses. It's the feature of this exercise. You need to push press a heavy kettlebell. Approximately 10 kg heavier than you press. If you military press a pair of 36 kg kettlebells, then you need to push press 44-48 kg kettlebell with one arm. Use schemes like 5x5 or 8x5. Muscles that are responsible for locking out work in the push press. It's common that people can make the kettlebell move, but come to a sticking point. That's when the push press can help you. Work with your pressing arm from start to end. Also, the kettlebell bench press can assist your military press development.

How frequently do you train?
Usually 3 times a week.

Thanks for the interview. It was very interesting and thought provoking.
Thanks. Good luck.

BONUS

You probably thought that this book was finally over. Not so fast, man. "Say hello to my little bonus" to rephrase the classics.

THE SANDBAG SWING

The swing is the most basic ballistic exercise you can perform. It is fun and it is effective. It develops explosive strength, your jumping ability and helps with fat loss through an increased calorie expenditure. Usually it is performed with one or a couple of kettlebells, but what should you do if you do not have even one? Take a sandbag.

How to Perform the Sandbag Swing

With the Sandbag Swing, the rules are the same as with the kettlebell version. You can see how it should be performed in the photos below:

You take a sandbag, swing it between your legs while simultaneously squatting, and reverse the move by exploding with your hips. Your arms should not bend throughout the move. In addition, it is not a Shoulder Raise, so you should not use your shoulder muscles as the main working force; the hips, back and legs should perform the majority of the work. In the perfect scenario, you should swing the bag up to eye level.

The main technique point here is to keep your lower back arched. This is the most powerful position, and it will prevent possible injuries.

If you squat deeper, you will feel it in the quads more. If you squat less — in the lower back.

Advantages and Limitations of the Drill

The primary concern in the Sandbag Swing should be the grip. You should crush the sandbag as hard as possible because it is way harder on the grip than the regular Kettlebell Swing. You do not want to break something valuable in your apartment due to the sandbag slipping out of your hands, right?

In addition, should you do it unilaterally or bilaterally? If you have two sandbags, you can try the two-armer. This variation will be more beneficial for building muscle and overall strength due to an increased workload comparing to the one-arm version. Here is some advice: I would not swing two sandbags *between* the legs; I would do it outside of them. Why? Because when the weight gets heavier and the bags are larger, there will not be enough space in between your legs.

What about the Sandbag Snatch? I could not find a way to do it properly with a simple non-commercial sandbag, so do not bother.

How to Incorporate It into Your Program?

Easily. Firstly, you should not put it before any exercises that require a solid grip. Therefore, the end of a training session seems the most reasonable for me. Secondly, it is a Lower Body Pull, so it should be treated as such. You can substitute Deadlift, Kettlebell Swing, Power Clean, and Sandbag Shouldering for this exercise. Thirdly, there are several options for where to put it in your actual program. If your goal is to gain muscle or to lose fat, then it should be performed at the end of a training session. Your grip will be fried afterwards, so you will not be able to show results in other exercises. If you use some sort of split, you should put it in the Back or Legs day. If you want to get good specifically in the Sandbag Swing, then I would put it on a separate day.

Example Workout

A) Handstand Push-Ups – 3 x 5
B) Double Kettlebell Bent-Over Rows – 3 x 6
C) One-Arm Sandbag Swing – 3 x 8 (per side)

Perform exercises in a straight fashion (finish all the sets of one before moving to the other). Rest around 3 minutes between sets and exercises. Once you can do all the reps in all the sets, increase the intensity.

How to Get Somewhat Crazy with the Sandbag Swing?

If you are brave enough, you can try alternating hands during the swings. All you should do is let go the bag at the top position with one hand and catch it with another. Perform this switch every rep. Soon you will obtain the fingers of steel.

Closing Thoughts

I guess this is everything you should know about the Sandbag Swing. Use it and get rid of lame excuses.

3 AWESOME LOW-TECH GRIP EXERCISES

I bet you thought this would be another article about Claw Fingertip Push-Ups, but it is not. I will give you three awesome low-tech grip exercises that can be easily performed at home. Here they are:

1. Towel Chin-Ups and Towel Curls

It seems that you can make any exercise fall into "grip strength" category by adding a regular towel to the mix. It is a simple, effective, and most importantly, no-cost solution to supercharge your grip in pulling exercises. There are two awesome ways to use towels in your training: Towel Chin-Ups and Towel Curls. The first one would be example of a multi-joint exercise, while the second one is an isolation move.

In Towel Chin-Ups, you basically hang one or two towels on a bar or rings, or a tree branch, grab them and perform the Chin-Ups.

In Towel Curls, you pass the towel through the hole in a weight plate, or through the handle of a kettlebell, and perform the Curls.

Both exercises can be applied to any program. Any Upper Body Pull can be substituted for Towel Chin-Ups. If you use split routine, then I would put them at the end of the Back day. Towel Curls can be used with success instead of any other type of curl. I have noticed that I feel my biceps WAY more in this exercise when compared to any other drill (excluding only the mighty One-Arm Chin-Up, but it is apples and oranges).

Regarding reps and sets, everything is up to you. I would use these exercises for higher reps, for example, 10-12.

2. Bottom-Up Kettlebell Clean and Press

Here is another great unconventional exercise to boost your grip strength. Just pick up the kettlebell, and clean and press it with its bottom up. It is as simple as that. Believe me, once the weight gets serious, you will struggle to perform even one rep.

I would not go higher than 10 reps in this exercise. However, it is all again up to you. Tip #1: chalk your hands. This will help you big time. Tip #2: if you cannot press a certain weight right away, do not get too upset. Work on Bottom-Up Cleans first. They are less demanding than the press. In addition, it will help you to get stronger grip and get used to the weight.

Where to put it in your program? I have experienced the best results in this exercise when I trained for it on a separate day. You should consider this. If you do not have extra time, then I would put it either in the beginning of the leg day in split routine, or in the end of the workout in the full-body program.

3. Sandbag One-Arm Lift

This one is so simple that you should be embarrassed not to have come up with it earlier. You fill the bag with sand, grab its tail (just like in the first Sandbag Swing picture), and lift it. That is it. Once you get to serious weights, your hands will beg for mercy.

You may find yourself in a situation where the sandbag is too high and it is impossible to lift it without bending your arm. Do not get too frustrated. Just stand on some bricks or chairs.

The Sandbag One-Arm Lift should always be placed at the end of the regular strength training session, unless you want to train it on a separate day. I would train it with low reps and a moderate amount of sets.

Closing Thoughts

Are these exercises the last word in grip training? Hell no. They give you variety and expand your mind on what you can do with everyday objects.

SOME THOUGHTS ON EXPLOSIVENESS

Explosive strength is an area that also requires improvement. It can effectively supplement your maximal strength training, or it can be used as a cool standalone method. So how can you develop it?

What Exercises to Choose?

For lower body explosive strength, let us look at the possessors of the highest vertical jump – the weightlifters. What exercises do they train to be able to generate so much explosive strength? They do not do much except the primary lifts: the Snatch and the Clean and Jerk. Therefore, for the lower body the possible exercises of choice are obvious. You can pick one from the list below:
- Barbell Snatch
- Kettlebell Snatch (One- and two-arm)
- Sandbag Shouldering
- Barbell Clean & Jerk
- Kettlebell Clean & Jerk (I would rather do the two-arm version)
- Sandbag Clean & Jerk

Getting stronger and, importantly, faster even in just one of those drills will be sufficient to develop great explosiveness in lower body.

What about the upper body? There are two basic movement patterns for the upper body where we can develop explosive strength: pushing and pulling. It is simplistic and not specific, I know. If you are an athlete who needs to get more explosive, the best thing you can do is to get stronger in explosive exercises that mimic your sport-specific situations. However, if you are a regular fitness enthusiast, then you do not need to bother.

For upper body pushing, I suggest the Clap Push-Ups. This exercise is simple, effective and requires no equipment. In this drill, you should push yourself up as fast and explosively as possible to be able to make a clap in between the reps. Once you get better with the regular version, you can either use additional weight, or move to a harder version (Behind the Back Clap Push-Up, Double Clap Push-Up, and Triple Clap Push-Up).

Other viable options for upper body pushing could be Clap Dips and Clap Handstand Push-Ups. These drills can be superior to Clap Push-Ups, but they require decent initial maximal strength. Remember, to work on explosiveness, you should be able to do at least 10-15 repetitions in the "non-clap" exercise. In addition, harder exercises can interfere with regular strength training. You are doing everything on purpose, right?

For upper body pulling, here are two obscure drills for you – Change Grip Pull-Ups and Clap Pull-Ups. First one is quite interesting and unconventional way to do Pull-Ups. It will require decent initial levels of strength though. This exercise is performed on the regular bar and starts just like ordinary Pull-Ups – with palms facing away. You pull yourself up as fast as possible from the dead hang, and at the top, you let go the bar and catch yourself with supinated grip (palms facing you). You should change your grip every rep.

With Clap Pull-Ups, everything is simpler. Pull yourself up as fast and explosively as possible, let go the bar, clap, and then catch yourself. I would not suggest you perform these with a grip where your palms are facing you.

In the end, I rarely see trainees incorporating explosive upper body pulling into their training routines, which can be the limiting factor for strength development in this movement pattern.

Another Way to Develop Explosiveness

If you want to develop explosive strength in specific movements, then here is a good option for you. Let us assume that you want to develop explosiveness in the Barbell Bench Press. What you can do is to load the bar to 60% of your one rep maximum and work on speed (pressing the bar as fast as possible). In addition, it can be a good idea to add bands and/or chains for extra resistance. This will supercharge your effort.

The method explained above is applicable to all the other weighted exercises too.

How to Incorporate Those Lifts in a Program?

First of all, you should understand that explosive strength is not the same thing as maximal strength or strength endurance. I wrote about it in the "How to Gain Strength" article. Therefore, muscular failure is not an indicator of training effect here, as well as increase in reps or working weight. An increase in the speed of the repetition with the same or greater weight can be considered an indicator of progress here. As a result, there is no need for high reps. The ideal rep protocol for developing explosive strength is 3-8 sets of 3 reps. I would put explosive work either on free days, or at the beginning of the workout. In addition, 3 sets of 3 in any explosive move can supercharge your nervous system better than any amount of caffeine.

Regarding amount of exercises, I would not do more than one per specific movement pattern. In addition, for majority of trainees, there is no need to train explosiveness more frequently than once a week.

Closing Thoughts

So should you develop explosiveness? If your goal is to build as much muscle as possible, then probably no. If your goal is to lose fat, there is also no vital need. However, if you want to have as much strength as possible and be fast, then I would consider adding 1-3 exercises to your training routine.

WHICH LOADED CARRIES TO ADD TO YOUR ROUTINE?

Loaded carries are really fun exercises, and are essential ways to develop strength in the whole body. What can be more essential than to carry something heavy around?

I would like to share with you several low-tech loaded carries you can perform anywhere.

1. Farmer's Walks

Everybody knows this exercise either from Brooks Kubik's "Dinosaur Training", or from watching almost any strongman competition. You pick up two heavy objects and carry them as long as you can. Usually this exercise is performed with either kettlebells or dumbbells, or special equipment for Farmer's Walks. While the last one is totally viable option that you will never outgrow, the first two will probably get easy really soon (unless you possess something exotic like an Inch Dumbbell). In this case, you can take two sandbags just like in the Sandbag Swing article earlier. This will keep you busy for some time.

However, what if that becomes too easy and you don't have the funds to buy a set of special equipment? Just pick the one of the options below.

2. Kettlebell Rack Walks

This carry will torch your core in addition to everything else. What you need to do is to pick up two kettlebells, clean them, and walk around in this position. You will be amazed how weak you are in this exercise compared to the Farmer's Walks.

3. Sandbag Zercher Carry

This exercise is similar to the one above, but you carry a sandbag in the Zercher position. You can expect much more soreness in biceps and traps compared to the Rack Walks.

4. Kettlebell Suitcase Carry

This exercise will unevenly load your body, which will lead to more core involvement, especially in the oblique area. It is performed exactly like the Farmer's Walks, but only with one kettlebell. If you are tired of regular carries, you can give this drill a shot.

5. Sandbag Bear Hug Carry

Bear Hug Carries are quite similar to the Zercher ones. However, you can handle more weight due to the position of the arms.

6. Overhead Walks

This is a bloody massacre. Pick the type of weight you prefer, clean it, and press it overhead. Now everything is set up; just walk around. Your arms and shoulders will beg for mercy really soon. If you work up to heavy weights, the stability in your shoulders will be amazing, and you will be able to press much more weight than you think.

7. Sandbag Shoulder Carry

Here is another great exercise with a sandbag. It is also simple. Shoulder a sandbag and walk around. That is it.

How to Incorporate Carries into a Program?

Here is some practical advice. If you train for general purposes (gaining muscle, losing fat), then you should add just one loaded carry at the end of the one of your training sessions. In several months, you can work up to 2-3 carries per week. If you plan to take part in strongman competitions and Farmer's Walks are the one of the disciplines, then you should emphasize them more. You may devote a whole training session for them.

Closing Thoughts

Should you add loaded carry to your routine? Definitely yes. Try it and let me know how it worked.

HOW TO AVOID WASTING TIME?

In modern society, there are lots of ways to waste time; way more than to spend it with purpose. People spend most of their day surfing the social networks for the information they do not really need. They spend their evenings drinking booze and smoking pot (some people spend their mornings like that). These people are always bored and looking for ways to entertain themselves (but in reality, THEY are the essence of their boredom). However, when they find a way to improve, they are depressed because of wasting so much time. For example, I know lots of people who wish they started training earlier, or there are lots of dudes and dudettes who wish they could start reading books earlier to be wiser and more-developed. There is an endless abyss of such examples.

So I would like to share with you ways how you can avoid wasting the most precious resource we have – time (training-wise and in general).

Search for Possible Mistakes

Just imagine that you are 10, 20, 30, 40 years older than now. What will you regret if your lifestyle remains the same? How bad would you feel if you still did not make that trip to [insert the country you want to visit]? How bad would you feel if you still did not make that parachute jump? How bad would you feel if you still did not record a solid music album? How bad would you feel if you still did not learn [insert the skill you always wanted to learn]? How bad would you feel if you still did not manage to build muscle and lose fat? I can go on and on.

That feeling described above sucks. That feeling will destroy you and break your will. It will silently kill you. The moment I imagine that feeling, I get so fucking unstoppable that I am ready to do literally anything to get to my goal.

The solution this problem is to search for possible mistakes in your current life that you will regret in the future, and **correct them**.

Set Goals for Yourself

Once you have found the possible mistakes, it is time to do something about it. It is easy if you want to read "War and Peace". Just read the piece. However, what to do if you have a nasty job that squeezes all the juices from you, a family with two kids and want to perform acrobatics at circus? This is hypothetical situation, but it is still possible. The answer is to set goals.

You should set daily, monthly and yearly goals for yourself. Every gigantic task can always be broken into much smaller ones. That is exactly what you need to do. If you want to write a book, it will be depressing to do it all at once. It is a lot of work. However, if you set a goal of writing 1000 words per day, which is achievable quite easily with consistency and perseverance, then you will be 1000 words closer to your dream each day. In several months, you will have a first draft. How awesome is that?

The same is true for strength training. Reaching the body of your dreams may be intimidating at first. However, if you understand that this is a daily process of eating right and training, then it is not that scary anymore. It will take as much as 3 hours per week for training, and some intelligent planning for food intake (which will take you and hour or two once a month).

Use 80/20 Principle

If you want to achieve your goals as fast as possible, you should use Pareto principle (80/20 rule) at least once or twice per month. This law is so awesome that you can apply it literally to everything. Regarding wasting time, it works like this: you pick the activities that you practice in order to reach your goals, find 20% that bring you 80% of results, and cut everything else. In case of strength training, you can find 20% of exercises that give you 80% of results, and cut everything else. In case of diet, you can find what 20% of techniques give you 80% of results, and forget about everything else. In the case of productivity, find 20% of daily activities that bring you 80% of results, and discard everything else.

Of course, it will not be easy to use this principle and to abandon activities you like. However, if you do this, you will get to your goals far quicker.

Closing Thoughts

I hope these techniques will help you not to waste the most expensive thing we have. Use your analytical skills, or at least develop them. This way your life will be much more fulfilling and effective.

HOW TO MAKE SMARTER FOOD CHOICES?

Making smarter food choices is not that hard as you may think. All it takes is to do some research regarding calories and macronutrients of the most common foods that you eat. As a result, you will be able to predict exactly how many calories are in any given food. To make the learning process simpler, you should divide all the foods into categories and create some rules. Here is my example:

1. Every food has a dominant macronutrient. For example, meat is mostly protein and fat, bread is mostly carbs, and olive oil is exclusively fat.

2. Fried foods have more calories. It happens through addition of oil, which has calories.

3. The fattier the piece of meat, the more fat will be in the end product. I usually cut off all the fat parts during the preparation. Meat is usually fatty by itself, so there is no need for additional calories.

4. Dressings count. You may think that if you use olive oil instead of mayonnaise, then your salad will be healthier. I encourage you to think again. Both of the dressings are primarily fat. 1g of fat has 9 calories. Do the math yourself. If your maintenance calories are low and you want to get leaner, then it will be better to use as little dressing as possible, if any. The same goes for different sauces. I am not saying that you should not use them. I am saying that you should be aware of additional calories.

5. Sugar counts. You may drink lots of tea and coffee with sugar throughout the day. Be aware that all the sugar counts. The same is true for all those beverages like coke and juices.

6. Protein foods:

- **Meat.** Meat is the most valuable thing you can put into your stomach (no matter what vegetarians and vegans say). It is essential for building muscle because it has lots of protein. Calorie counters will give you quite a wide range for amount of calories in different kinds of meat. However, usually it is ~250-300 calories for fried pork and beef. Regarding macronutrients, they are: protein – ~25g per 100g; carbs – 0g, fat – check out point #3.

- **Poultry.** Poultry is also should be a food of choice for diet-conscious people. It has less fat than meat and more protein, which is great. Fried chicken breast has ~200 calories and ~30g of protein.

- **Eggs.** Eggs are a cheap source of protein and fat, and they taste great. I was eating up to 13 of these bad boys per day some time ago. However, despite the low price they are not optimal as exclusive protein source due to high fat content. Usually one egg is ~100 calories and has ~7g of protein.

- **Cottage cheese.** Cottage cheese is another great example of protein food. To keep everything simple, I usually buy it at grocery store. As a result, the product has printed weight and nutrition facts on the package. The less fat it has, the more protein is there, but the more it tastes like shit. Fat-free cottage cheese has a depressing taste, but it has 41g of protein per 193 calories (230g package), which is ~85% (it is better than in most protein powder supplements out there). Nevertheless, I found a way to make it taste ultimately better. I add a pinch of salt and a half-tablespoon of sugar (I know that I told to avoid it, but in this particular case, it is the only way to make it taste like food, not shit).

7. Carb foods:

- **Grains and pasta.** As a rule, grains and pasta contain lots of carbs, ~10g of protein per 100g, almost no fats, and ~350 calories. These numbers are relevant for the dry grains and pasta; cooked ones will have half of that per 100g.

- **Potatoes.** Potatoes are similar to grains, but have less calories and carbs.

- **Bread.** Bread is similar to the ones above. It has ~200 calories per 100g.

- **Fruits.** Despite what others may tell you, fruits are not the same as vegetables. They contain quite a lot of calories and carbs, so you cannot eat them in unlimited amounts. Search Google for additional info.

8. Fat foods. I rarely eat purely fat foods. The meat and eggs contain enough fats to support my diet.

9. Vegetables. I prefer not to count them. I guess you can eat any amount of tomatoes, cucumbers, spinach, broccoli, and others with no adverse consequences.

10. Always focus on protein. When you choose your food, you can never go wrong with the protein section above.

11. Cookies, cakes, and other sweets contain low-to-no protein, and lots of fats and carbs. The right conclusion is to avoid such foods.

12. One bottle of beer has around 200 calories and 42g of carbs.

13. One gram of pure alcohol is 7 calories. Remember that vodka, tequila, and gin have calories too.

NOTE: *all the numbers are taken from calorie-counters and Google. They are shown for example purposes. I encourage you to make your own research.*

Closing Thoughts

Predicting calories and macronutrient profile in most of the food I eat is quite easy for me now (after all these years). If you develop a similar set of rules, making smarter food choices will be much easier for you. With time, you will just look at the available food and understand what can be useful and what cannot.

P.S. I still cannot predict the weight of the portion, so I use the kitchen scales for this.

CLOSING THOUGHTS

So you have reached the last part. It took a lot of effort for me to finish this book, and I hope you find it useful and entertaining.

What I want you to understand is that while the book has ended, your Rough Strength journey has just begun. If you refuse to obey modern fitness trends, now you have all the weapons you need. You can show the middle finger and say goodbye to commercial gyms, supplements, gurus, "programs of champions", exercise machines, fancy gym clothes, gym socialization, all the mentally deficient people who train abs all day and waste your time with their moronic questions, and finally get those results you always wanted.

Remember, you can be on the road to success with anything you have at hand. It can take as little equipment as your bodyweight, a sandbag and a couple of kettlebells.

Focus on what is important and discard everything else. Do not waste time on unimportant things, and you will accomplish your goals WAY quicker.

Stick to the plan. Do not jump from program to program weekly. Do not jump from one diet approach to another weekly. Do not jump from one training implement to another weekly. Everything requires time. If you find something that delivers results, stick to it as long as it is working.

Be patient and do not rush things. Impatience breeds ignorance and failure. Everything has its own speed. The processes in your body can have only two speeds: optimal and sub-optimal. If you rush things, it will be the latter.

Make the necessary sacrifices to get what you desire. Drop watching TV at night if it interferes with your sleep. Drop eating cookies if it interferes with your diet and fat loss. Drop anything that interferes with your training.

Do not forget about hard work. All the valuable things you will ever get in life will be results of hard work. And the harder the work, the more satisfying the reward will be.

Never stop educating yourself. Read more. I have a lot of homework for you in the "Recommended Reading" section.

And one more thing. I have a request for you. If you like this book, e-mail it to a person who can benefit from it. Right now.

That is it.

Play rough!

Alex

P.S. So why exactly 42 articles? You may be beating walls with your head to guess, but, actually, there is no reason. I just did not want it to be ordinary. Besides, isn't "42" the meaning of life?

ACKNOWLEDGMENTS

Now it is the perfect time to say thank you.

The first 'thank you' goes to my wife Alina for the immense support and not killing me in my sleep because of all the hard times during the writing of this book. In addition, thanks for enduring the hardship of taking the photos. In case you do not know, she is the author of the most of the photos on the Rough Strength blog.

Thanks to my parents for making me who I am.

Thanks to Ramon Davila for proofreading the book and correcting my poor English.

Thanks to Paul Wade for inspiration and writing the awesome foreword.

Thanks to all the Rough Strength fans for showing me that the things I have to say are interesting and useful. This book would not be released without your support.

Thanks to Vadym Sapatrylo for shooting the awesome book trailer. Check out more works by this badass here [25].

Thanks to all the people who shared their knowledge with me throughout these years.

And thank you, my friend, for reading this far. You have just got better.

RECOMMENDED READING

Here I will share with you the information sources I find useful. There is no particular order.

"Starting Strength" by Mark Rippetoe
If you are just starting strength training, it is the best program you can follow.

"Dinosaur Training" by Brooks Kubik
If you are stuck in the high-volume bodybuilding "programs of champions", this will be the perfect read.

"Convict Conditioning" by Paul Wade
If you are still in doubt about calisthenics, read this book for inspiration.

"Never Gymless" by Ross Enamait
If you think that bodyweight training is a waste of time, this will be a good book to read.

"Overcoming Gravity" by Steven Low
If you seek in-depth advice on bodyweight strength training, this can be a good read.

LeanGains Blog by Martin Berkhan - http://www.leangains.com/
If you struggle to lose fat, gain muscle, and never heard about intermittent fasting, this blog will keep you busy for some time.

"Beyond Bodybuilding" by Pavel Tsatsouline

If you want unconventional advice on building your body, this is a good read.

"Building the Gymnastic Body" by Christopher Sommer

If you want to learn more about gymnastics training, check this book out.

Jason Ferruggia's Blog - http://jasonferruggia.com/

If you want to learn more simple information about strength training, check it out.

Lucharilla - http://www.lucharilla.com/

If you want to learn more about reasonable programming, I encourage you to read this blog.

"Aggressive Strength Solution for Size and Strength" by Mike Mahler

If you want to learn more about using kettlebells for strength development, read this book.

"The Warrior Diet" & "Maximum Muscle Minimum Fat" by Ori Hofmekler

If you want to learn another reasonable approach to dieting, read these pieces.

"Brawn" & "Beyond Brawn" by Stuart McRobert

If you want to read more about no-bullshit approach to strength training, I suggest you to check out these books.

"Burn the Fat, Feed the Muscle" by Tom Venuto

If you want to learn the basics of dieting, this should be a great read.

"The One-Arm Chinning Guide" by Jack Arnow and Alexander Lechner - http://www.dragondoor.com/articles/the-one-arm-chinning-guide/

It is self-explanatory.

Iron Addict's Forum - http://www.ironaddicts.com/forums

If you want to learn more real-world strength training and nutrition information, you should definitely follow this link.

Zach Even-Esh's Blog - http://zacheven-esh.com/blogs/
It is another great blog that deserves to be read.

Beast Skills - http://www.beastskills.com/
If you want to find great tutorials on bodyweight skills, look no further.

Charles Poliquin's Articles - http://www.poliquingroup.com/ArticlesMultimedia/Articles.aspx
It is another great source of training information.

"A Guide to Flexible Dieting" by Lyle McDonald
If you want to learn how to stay sane during dieting, read this book.

"My Mad Methods" Magazine
If you want to learn more about training with unconventional implements, check this source out.

Rough Strength Blog by Alex Zinchenko – http://roughstrength.com
If you want to be awesome, you should check this one out. Frequently. In addition, subscribe to the awesome newsletter [26], as well as join me on Facebook [27] and Twitter [28].

WARNING! It is shameless advertisement, but who cares.
Check out my music here [29] and subscribe to this blog [18]. And, of course, join the Facebook page [30].

That should be enough for now.

ABOUT THE AUTHOR

Alex Zinchenko is a strength addict, coach and author of the Rough Strength blog [1], where he shares his crazy ideas regarding training and nutrition. He is honest to toothache, straightforward like a train, and too daring to believe that heavy calisthenics, kettlebell and sandbag training along with intermittent fasting can deliver all the results you want.

You can contact him through the e-mail: roughstrengthmailbox@gmail.com

In addition, get in touch on Facebook [27] and Twitter [28].

REFERENCES

1) http://roughstrength.com/

2) http://youtu.be/2SSCPfqGlXM

3) http://gymnasticswod.com/content/s00177?size=medium

4) http://youtu.be/ChQha6QgdvI

5) http://youtu.be/scD9yFUez-I

6) http://youtu.be/53x96OAQFjI

7) http://roughstrength.com/convict-conditioning-and-my-thoughts/

8) http://youtu.be/G1-J_hcJC5c

9) http://www.t-nation.com/free_online_article/sports_body_training_performance/inside_the_muscles_best_back_and_biceps_exercises&cr=

10) https://www.facebook.com/yuvalonhands

11) http://youtu.be/quC8faQJKIs

12) http://youtu.be/VKz0aSoL9Hk

13) http://youtu.be/dRKP2rjO4AE

14) http://youtu.be/6TlbDQUWs0s

15) http://youtu.be/4mtd_IuiQR0

16) http://www.leangains.com/2011/05/omega-3-fatty-acids-for-muscle-growth.html

17) http://youtu.be/RSedc1w6d8s

18) http://stonefromthesky.blogspot.com/

19) http://www.t-nation.com/free_online_article/sports_body_training_performance/in_defense_of_overhead_lifting

20) http://youtu.be/RcQogAS5638

21) http://youtu.be/y4Wo095zPnc

22) http://youtu.be/NuzGMud0MXE

23) http://youtu.be/9GjEsqqYHYk

24) http://youtu.be/WuVNnVABGxE

25) https://vimeo.com/sapatrylo

26) http://roughstrength.com/getting-started/

27) https://www.facebook.com/roughstrengthofficial

28) https://twitter.com/roughstrength

29) https://soundcloud.com/stonefromthesky

30) https://www.facebook.com/stonefromthesky

Made in the USA
San Bernardino, CA
05 June 2014